THE ISLAMIC TRILOGY

VOLUME 2

THE POLITICAL TRADITIONS
OF MOHAMMED

THE HADITH
FOR THE UNBELIEVERS

BILL WARNER, PHD

THE ISLAMIC TRILOGY SERIES

VOLUME 1

MOHAMMED AND THE UNBELIEVERS

VOLUME 2

THE POLITICAL TRADITIONS OF MOHAMMED

VOLUME 3

A SIMPLE KORAN

VOLUME 4

AN ABRIDGED KORAN

WWW.CSPIPUBLISHING.COM

THE ISLAMIC TRILOGY

VOLUME 2

THE POLITICAL TRADITIONS

OF MOHAMMED

THE HADITH
FOR THE UNBELIEVERS

BILL WARNER, PHD

CENTER FOR THE STUDY
OF POLITICAL ISLAM

CSPI PUBLISHING

THE ISLAMIC TRILOGY

VOLUME 2

THE POLITICAL TRADITIONS
OF MOHAMMED

THE HADITH
FOR THE UNBELIEVERS

BILL WARNER, PHD

ISBN 0-9785528-7-3
ISBN13 978-0-9785528-7-9
PERFECT BOUND
V 10.13.2016

CSPI PUBLISHING
WWW.CSPIPUBLISHING.COM

TABLE OF CONTENTS

PREFACE

The Center for the Study of Political Islam, CSPI, teaching method is the easiest and quickest way to learn about Islam.

Authoritative

There are only two ultimate authorities about Islam—Allah and Mohammed. All of the curriculum in the CSPI method is from the Koran and the Sunna (the words and deeds of Mohammed). The knowledge you get in CSPI is powerful, authoritative and irrefutable. You learn the facts about the ideology of Islam from its ultimate sources.

Story-telling

Facts are hard to remember, stories are easy to remember. The most important story in Islam is the life of Mohammed. Once you know the story of Mohammed, all of Islam is easy to understand.

Systemic Knowledge

The easiest way to study Islam is to first see the whole picture. The perfect example of this is the Koran. The Koran alone cannot be understood, but when the life of Mohammed is added, the Koran is straight forward.

There is no way to understand Islam one idea at the time, because there is no context. Context, like story-telling, makes the facts and ideas simple to understand. The best analogy is that when the jig saw puzzle is assembled, the image on the puzzle is easy to see. But looking at the various pieces, it is difficult to see the picture.

Levels of Learning

The ideas of Islam are very foreign to our civilization. It takes repetition to grasp the new ideas. The CSPI method uses four levels of training to teach the doctrine in depth. The first level is designed for a beginner. Each level repeats the basics for in depth learning.

When you finish the first level you will have seen the entire scope of Islam, The in depth knowledge will come from the next levels.

Political Islam, Not Religious Islam

Islam has a political doctrine and a religious doctrine. Its political doctrine is of concern for everyone, while religious Islam is of concern only for Muslims.

Books Designed for Learning

Each CSPI book fits into a teaching system. Most of the paragraphs have an index number which means that you can confirm for yourself how factual the books are by verifying from the original source texts.

LEVEL 1

INTRODUCTION TO THE TRILOGY AND SHARIA

The Life of Mohammed, The Hadith, Lectures on the Foundations of Islam, The Two Hour Koran, Sharia Law for Non-Muslims, Self Study on Political Islam, Level 1

LEVEL 2

APPLIED DOCTRINE, SPECIAL TOPICS

The Doctrine of Women, The Doctrine of Christians and Jews, The Doctrine of Slavery, Self-Study on Political Islam, Level 2, Psychology of the Muslim, Factual Persuasion

LEVEL 3

INTERMEDIATE TRILOGY AND SHARIA

Mohammed and the Unbelievers, Political Traditions of Mohammed, Simple Koran, Self-Study of Political Islam, Level 3, Sources of the Koran, selected topics from *Reliance of the Traveller*

LEVEL 4

ORIGINAL SOURCE TEXTS

The Life of Muhammed, Guillaume; any *Koran, Sahih Bukhari,* selected topics, *Mohammed and Charlemagne Revisited,* Scott.

With the completion of Level 4 you are prepared to read both popular and academic texts.

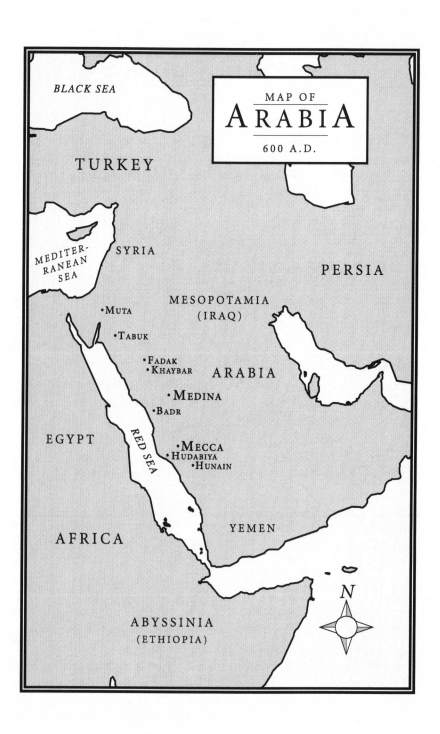

MAP OF
ARABIA
600 A.D.

BLACK SEA

TURKEY

MEDITER-
RANEAN
SEA

SYRIA

PERSIA

•MUTA

MESOPOTAMIA
(IRAQ)

•TABUK

•FADAK
•KHAYBAR

ARABIA

•MEDINA
•BADR

EGYPT

RED SEA

•MECCA
•HUDABIYA
•HUNAIN

AFRICA

YEMEN

N

ABYSSINIA
(ETHIOPIA)

INTRODUCTION

The first step in learning about Islam is to know the right words. The language of Islam is dualistic. There is a division of humanity into believer and *kafir* (unbeliever). Humanity is divided into those who believe Mohammed is the prophet of Allah and those who do not.

Kafir is the actual word the Koran uses for non-Muslims. It is usually translated as unbeliever, but that translation is wrong. The word unbeliever is neutral. As you will see, the attitude of the Koran towards unbelievers is very negative. The Koran defines the Kafir.

In Islam, Christians and Jews are infidels and "People of the Book"; Hindus are polytheists and pagans. The terms infidel, People of the Book, pagan and polytheist are religious words. Only the word "Kafir" shows the common political treatment of the Christian, Jew, Hindu, Buddhist, animist, atheist and humanist. What is done to a pagan can be done to a Jew or any other Kafir. Likewise, what is done to a Jew can be done to any other Kafir.

The word Kafir will be used in this book instead of "unbeliever", "non-Muslim" or "disbeliever". Unbeliever or non-Muslim are neutral terms, but Kafir is extremely bigoted and biased.

The Kafir is hated—

> 40:35 *They [Kafirs] who dispute the signs [Koran verses] of Allah without authority having reached them are greatly hated by Allah and the believers. So Allah seals up every arrogant, disdainful heart.*

A Kafir can be enslaved [Bukhari is a sacred text, see "Introduction to the Hadith" on page ix.]—

> Bukhari 5,58,148 *When some of the remaining Jews of Medina agreed to obey a verdict from Saed, Mohammed sent for him. He approached the Mosque riding a donkey and Mohammed said, "Stand up for your leader." Mohammed then said, "Saed, give these people your verdict." Saed replied, "Their soldiers should be beheaded and their women and children should become slaves." Mohammed, pleased with the verdict, said, "You have made a ruling that Allah or a king would approve of."*

A Kafir can be raped—
> 1759 *On the occasion of Khaybar, Mohammed put forth new orders about forcing sex with captive women. If the woman was pregnant she was not to be used for sex until after the birth of the child. Nor were any women to be used for sex who were unclean with regard to Muslim laws about menstruation.*

A Kafir can be beheaded—
> 47:4 *When you encounter the Kafirs on the battlefield, cut off their heads until you have thoroughly defeated them and then take the prisoners and tie them up firmly.*

A Kafir can be confused—
> 6:25 *Some among them listen to you [Mohammed], but We have cast veils over their [Kafirs'] hearts and a heaviness to their ears so that they cannot understand our signs [the Koran].*

A Kafir can be plotted against—
> 86:15 *They plot and scheme against you [Mohammed], and I plot and scheme against them. Therefore, deal calmly with the Kafirs and leave them alone for a while.*

A Kafir can be terrorized—
> 8:12 *Then your Lord spoke to His angels and said, "I will be with you. Give strength to the believers. I will send terror into the Kafirs' hearts, cut off their heads and even the tips of their fingers!"*

A Kafir can be made war on and humiliated—
> 9:29 *Make war on those who have received the Scriptures [Jews and Christians] but do not believe in Allah or in the Last Day. They do not forbid what Allah and His Messenger have forbidden. The Christians and Jews do not follow the religion of truth until they submit and pay the poll tax [jizya], and they are humiliated.*

A Muslim is not the friend of a Kafir—
> 3:28 *Believers should not take Kafirs as friends in preference to other believers. Those who do this will have none of Allah's protection and will only have themselves as guards. Allah warns you to fear Him for all will return to Him.*

THE THREE VIEWS OF ISLAM

There are three points of view in dealing with Islam. The point of view depends upon how you feel about Mohammed. If you believe Mohammed is the prophet of Allah, then you are a believer. If you don't, you are a *Kafir*. The third viewpoint is that of a Kafir who is an apologist for Islam.

Apologists do not believe that Mohammed was a prophet, but they never say anything that would displease a Muslim. Apologists never offend Islam and condemn any analysis that is critical of Islam as being biased.

Let us give an example of the three points of view.

In Medina, Mohammed sat all day long beside his 12-year-old wife while they watched as the heads of 800 Jews were removed by sword.[1] Their heads were cut off because they had said that Mohammed was not the prophet of Allah.

Muslims view these deaths as necessary because denying Mohammed's prophet-hood was an offense against Islam and beheading is the accepted method of punishment, sanctioned by Allah.

- Kafirs look at this event as proof of the jihadic violence of Islam and as an evil act.
- Apologists say that this was a historic event, that all cultures have violence in their past, and that no judgment should be passed. According to the different points of view, killing the 800 Jews was either evil, a perfect godly act or only another historical event, take your pick.
- Apologists ignore the Islamic belief that the Sunna, Mohammed's words and deeds in the past, is the perfect model for today and tomorrow and forever. They ignore the fact that this past event of the beheading of 800 Jewish men continues to be acceptable in the present and the future, thus the fate of Kafirs today.

This book is written from the Kafir point of view and is therefore, Kafir-centric. Everything in this book views Islam from how it affects Kafirs, non-Muslims. This also means that the religion is of little importance. Only a Muslim cares about the religion of Islam, but all Kafirs are affected by Islam's political views.

Both the apologists and the Muslims believe in an authoritarian philosophy of knowledge. The Muslim accepts without question every aspect of the Sunna and the Koran. The apologist bows to the authority and opinion of the Muslims and never contradicts them.

The Kafir approach to knowledge is analytic or critical. Critical thinking seeks truth through the friction of debate in order to tease out the resolution of an idea. Authoritarians forbid critical thought for the simple reason that it cannot co-exist with authoritative thinking. Muslims forbid critical thinking by threatening and inducing fear. Apologists forbid critical thinking on

---

1   *The Life of Muhammad*, A. Guillaume, Oxford University Press, 1982, pg. 464.

the basis that offending any minority is a social evil. The offending speech is considered bigoted. The proof of bigotry is that the minority is offended. Even if the statement is true, it can still be called bigotry.

"Truth" has no meaning in authoritative knowledge. There are only thoughts that are allowed and thoughts that are forbidden. "Truth" is determined by appeal to authority, but only to the correct authority. Authoritative knowledge forbids debate. Those who want to debate are demeaned and insulted or simply locked out of the venue. Both political correctness and Islam agree that only "allowed" opinions may be expressed and "forbidden" opinions are declared to be bigotry—a moral evil.

Critical thinking, however, exists by debate. There are no forbidden ideas in critical or analytic thinking.

Notice that these different points of view that cannot be reconciled. There is no possible resolution between the view of the Kafir and the Muslim. The apologist tries to bring about a bridge building compromise, but it is not logically possible.

THE ISLAMIC BIBLE—THE TRILOGY

Islam is defined by the words of Allah in the Koran, and the words and actions of Mohammed, the *Sunna*.

The Sunna of Mohammed is found in two texts—the Sira (Mohammed's life) and the Hadith. His words and actions are considered to be the divine pattern for humanity acceptable to Allah and the best source for these are the biographies, or Sira, by Ishaq and Al Tabari.

A hadith, or tradition, is a brief story about what Mohammed did or said. A collection of hadiths is called a Hadith. There are many collections of hadiths, but the most authoritative are those by Bukhari and Abu Muslim.

So the Trilogy is the Koran, the Sira and the Hadith. Most people think that the Koran is the "bible" of Islam, but it is only about 14% of the total textual doctrine. Statistically, Islam is 14% Allah and 86% Mohammed. The Trilogy, not the Koran, is the foundation of Islamic doctrine.

INTRODUCTION TO THE HADITH

A hadith, or tradition, usually only a paragraph long, is an action, brief story, or conversation about or by Mohammed. The action can be as elementary as Mohammed's drinking a glass of water or putting on his sandals. A collection of these stories is called the Hadith or Traditions. So the Hadith is a collection of hadiths (the actual plural of hadith is *ahadith*).

The Hadith contains the *Sunna* (the ideal speech or action) of Mohammed, that is, his pronouncements. The actual words or deeds, then, that one should follow, are the Sunna; the story that gave rise to the Sunna is the hadith.

There are many collectors of hadiths, but the two most authoritative collectors were Muhammad Ibn Ismail Al-Bukhari, or Bukhari, and Abu Al-Husayn Muslim, or Muslim. Most of the hadiths in this book come from Bukhari. From 600,000 hadiths, he took the most reliable and recorded them in *Sahih of Al-Bukhari*, also known as *Sahih Bukhari*. Muslim's work is called *Sahih Muslim*.

Bukhari recorded about one hadith in a hundred and threw out ninety-nine percent of the rest because he found them unreliable, due to political enhancement or romantic storytelling. Like all the other writings about Mohammed, they were recorded about two hundred years after he died. That would be similar to writing George Washington's first biography today, and the writer would have to derive his facts from stories recounted in popular, cultural entertainment. In keeping with good storytelling, the stories would have grown over time and details would have been added and embellished with each telling.

There was another complication for Bukhari—politics. Since all Islamic politics are based upon what Mohammed did and said, stories could be found showing that Mohammed did or said whatever would prove a particular political view. When a ruler needed a hadith to prove a political point, the ruler got a hadith.

The way that Bukhari sorted out the hadiths was to use a chain of evidence. Whenever he heard a hadith from someone, he would try to determine where that person heard the hadith and from whom he or she heard it. The chain of evidence, called an *isnad*, had to go back to Mohammed's time. At the beginning of the chain, there had to be someone who was known to be reliable who had heard it from Mohammed or one of his companions. Some of Bukhari's isnads were a long chain of evidence going back five to ten generations. (Since the isnads are useful only to scholars, they are not referenced here because this is an introductory text.)

There are many other collections of hadiths. Four more collections, in addition to those of Bukhari and Muslim, round out the collection of six Hadiths called the "Six Musannaf." There are many other collections that are not as revered as these six, but Bukhari and Muslim are considered the most reliable.

The Shia Muslims use another set of hadiths; however, since the Shia are but a small part of Islam, their Hadith will not be dealt with here.

A few of the hadiths are not about Mohammed but about Ali, Umar, Abu Bakr, and Uthman. These four men were Mohammed's closest companions and became caliphs—absolute religious and political rulers of Islam and the equivalent of religious kings. They are called "the rightly guided caliphs," and their Sunna (words and actions) are also considered ideal Islamic behavior.

All of the hadiths in this work have many duplicates or near duplicates—like multiple witnesses recounting the same event. They blend seamlessly with the Koran and the Sira. They do not contradict any of the Islamic doctrine. They are from the most trusted sources of hadiths— Bukhari and Muslim.

WHAT ARE THE DIFFICULTIES?

The Hadith are difficult to read and understand because:
- There is endless repetition of the same information.
- Most of the material is only of interest to a Muslim, e.g. how to pray.
- It is so long that it is discouraging to read.
- The English translation is awkward.
- The Hadith are obscure to Kafirs.

Bukhari's Hadith is vast, but the large number of hadiths is an illusion. If you were to go through the collection and combine all of the hadiths that describe the same scene, there are probably fewer than a thousand hadiths that are unique. It is interesting that no one has ever done this tedious, but straightforward editing task. Muslims don't do it because it would make the doctrine much easier to understand. Islam substitutes complexity for profoundness. A simplified Hadith would make the imam less necessary and give him less power. The entire Trilogy is designed to be difficult to understand.

CLARIFICATION

Since there are so many hadiths that report the same event with minor differences, it is obvious that all the hadiths that relate the same event need to be collected and a summary hadith be written.

The second simplification is to primarily deal with the hadiths that affect Kafirs. About 70% of the hadiths are about the minutia of being a Muslim, such as how to pray. For the Kafir, these hadiths may be amusing, but most of them are tedious and foreign to us. It is the politics of the Hadith, how Islam treats the Kafir, that is important to us. Remember this book is Kafir-centric. The text by Bukhari devotes 21% to jihad , 9% to the

Jews and 3% to Christians. This means we only need to understand about a third of the Hadith. There are about 2000 hadiths about Kafirs and since there is great repetition, there are only a few hundred hadiths that need to be scrutinized in a Kafir-centric study. This is very manageable.

The Hadiths Are Written In Clumsy English.

There is only one translation of Bukhari and Muslim into English and it is very clear that the translators were not native speakers of English. The hadiths here have been rewritten for clarity. Here is an example of how their translations have been made clearer. First, the original:

So the Prophet faced the Kabah and the fools amongst the people namely "the Jews" said, "What has turned them from their kiblah (Bait-ul-Maqdis) which they formerly observed?"

Here is the rewritten passage:

So Mohammed faced Mecca and prayed and the fools among the people, namely the Jews, said, "What caused you to stop praying while facing Jerusalem?"

This is very straightforward task for an editor.

WHAT IS THIS BOOK?

Selections have been made from thousands of hadiths from Bukhari and Muslim and have been sorted into categories. There is a large amount of repetition because the same story may be told as many as eight times by eight different people. It is rare to find a hadith that is not a duplicate.

Many of these hadiths concern political Islam, in other words, how Islam treats Kafirs. Many of the hadiths are about religious rituals. Mohammed prayed frequently, and the details of his prayer could be recorded as a hadith. The other ritual event that is recorded in detail concerns ablutions (ritual bathing). Some acts are ritually unclean, for example, urination or sex. After an unclean act, an ablution must be performed so a Muslim can enter a state of ritual purity in order to pray or pick up a Koran, for instance. Many different hadiths of ritual purity were preserved.

Since this book is about political Islam, few of these ritual purity and prayer hadiths are found here, but some of them have been included because they are interesting.

We know more about Mohammed's personal habits than those of any other man in history. How he put on his shoes or entered the bathroom was recorded so he could be a model for all humanity for all times.

Most repetitions of the same event have been left out. Some repetitions have been kept if a hadith illustrates principles in more than one topic. For instance, the same hadith about a black, female slave could be used in the subjects of women, slavery, and race. Some are repeated for the same reason that they are kept in the original Hadith. Each one shows a slightly different emphasis or an added detail.

Lastly, these hadiths are the very foundation of the Sharia, Islamic law; furthermore, there is no Islam without politics, so the lesson of the Hadith, the Sira, and the Koran is that Islam must rule all politics. The belief is that, since Islamic politics come straight from the only god, it is only a matter of time before political Islam prevails over all.

These hadiths are sacred literature. The Koran repeatedly tells all Muslims to copy the divine pattern of Mohammed's actions and words. For Islam, Mohammed is the model political leader, husband, warrior, philosopher, religious leader, and neighbor. Mohammed is the ideal pattern of man for all times and all places.

One way to view this book is as a map of the original texts. Once you have read this book, you will be able to read and understand the source texts.

WHAT ARE THE RESULTS?

Once all of the underbrush is cleared, some things stand out. The Hadith are filled with animosity toward Jews. The reason for this is the majority of the hadiths come from the Medinan period. In Mecca the Jews are portrayed positively. In Medina, Islam portrays the Jews in an extremely negative way.

It is also clear that some of the hadiths contradict each other. Islam is built on a foundation of contradictions. When Bukhari produced his Hadith, the only criteria were the chain of transmitters, not the content of the hadith. Many of the contradictory hadiths support one political view or the other. Remember that Islam is a political ideology, so it is not surprising that the hadith will be politically biased.

The Hadith not only flesh out the Koran and give the details of how to be a Muslim, but also, in some cases, they contradict the Koran. Now, this would seem to be an easy problem to solve. Surely the Koran trumps the Hadith, but it is not so. As an example, the Koran refers to prayer three times a day, but the Hadith gives the number as five times a day. Five is the number the Muslims accept, not three.

There is another major problem for some Muslims in the Hadith. The Hadith document brutality by Mohammed and the Muslims. Mohammed ordered that some thieves have their hands and feet removed, hot nails put in their eyes and that they be left to die from thirst in the hot sun lying on sharp rocks. In other hadiths, he gives the rules for raping captured women.

In a modern world, some Muslim scholars reject this picture of Mohammed and condemn the entire idea of the Hadith. So they argue that Islam should depend only upon the Koran. The problem with this idea is that the Koran does not give enough information on how to practice Islam. If you throw out the Hadith, you can't practice Islam. So you have to accept some of the Hadith.

If you ever bring up a hadith that Muslims do not like, they say: "Well, some of those hadiths are not reliable." This magic incantation, "some hadiths are not reliable" can be used whenever necessary. However, if you are quoting from Bukhari, this is a failing argument, since it is the *crème de la crème*, the ultimate collection.

This deniability is part of the dualism of Islam. Dualism lets Muslims choose which side of a contradiction to use and not deny the truth of the other side of the contradiction, so one Muslim can say that a particular hadith is not "reliable" while another Muslim can use it. In Islam you can have your cake and eat it too. Dualism is one of the two fundamental principles of Islam and will be dealt with in its own chapter.

REFERENCE NUMBERS

The information in this book can be traced back to the source by use of the reference numbers:

I234 is a reference to Ibn Ishaq's *Sirat Rasul Allah*, translated by A. Guillaume as The Life of Muhammad. This is a reference to margin note 234.

T123 is a reference to *The History of al-Tabari* by the State University of New York. The number refers to the margin note 123.

M234 is a reference to *The Life of Mohammed* by Sir William Muir, AMS Press, New York, NY, 1975. The number is page 234.

B2,3,45 is a reference to *Sahih Bukhari*, Bukhari's Hadith. The three example numbers are volume 2, book 3, and number 45, a standard reference system.

M2,345 is a reference to *Sahih Muslim*, Muslim's Hadith. The example would be book 2, number 345.

12:45 is Koran chapter (sura) 12, verse 45.

SPELLING

It is the present state of knowledge of the West about Islam that there is no standardized spelling of proper Arabic nouns. Examples: Muslim/Moslem, Mohammed/Muhammad, Koran/Quran.

ETHICS

CHAPTER 1

*9:63 Do they not know that whoever opposes Allah
and His Messenger will abide in the fire of Hell, where
they will remain forever? This is the great shame.*

You would do well to read the Introduction.

Outsiders judge a religion by its ethics. They are not concerned with what it teaches about salvation or life after death, but they care greatly what the religion tells members about outsiders. The foundation of this interaction between adherents and non-members is ethics.

The Hadith is filled with details of the ethics of Islam.

BROTHERHOOD

The brother of a Muslim is another Muslim.

B1,2,12 Mohammed: "True faith comes when a man's personal desires mirror his wishes for other Muslims."

B8,73,99 Mohammed: "Worshipers of Allah, do not allow hatred or jealousy to divide you. Live as brothers. It is sacrilege for one Muslim to desert his brother or to refuse to speak with him for three successive nights."

B9,85,83 Mohammed: "A Muslim is a brother to other Muslims. He should never oppress them nor should he facilitate their oppression. Allah will satisfy the needs of those who satisfy the needs of their brothers."

B3,34,366 Jarir gave an oath to Mohammed that he would always proclaim that there is no god but Allah and Mohammed is His prophet. He also promised to follow all prayer rituals, pay his taxes, hear and obey Allah's and Mohammed's commands, and never give bad advice to another Muslim.

HONESTY

A Muslim should always be honest in dealing with other Muslims.

B3,34,301 A man selling wares in the market place swore by Allah that he had been offered a certain price for his goods when, in fact, no such offer existed. He lied about the offer to drive up the price for his goods and thus cheat a fellow Muslim. Consequently, this verse in the Koran was revealed to Mohammed:

> 3:77 *Those who sell their covenant with Allah and their oaths for a meager price will have no part in the world to come. Allah will not find them worthy to speak to or even glance in their direction on the Day of Resurrection, nor will He forgive them. They will have a painful end.*

B1,2,54 Jarir promised Mohammed that he would strictly follow prayer ritual, pay his taxes to help the needy, and be faithful and truthful to all Muslims.

TRUTH

In Islam something that is not true is not always a lie.

B3,49,857 Mohammed: "A man who brings peace to the people by making up good words or by saying nice things, though untrue, does not lie."

An oath by a Muslim is flexible.

B8,78,618 Abu Bakr faithfully kept his oaths until Allah revealed to Mohammed the atonement for breaking them. Afterwards he said, "If I make a pledge and later discover a more worthy pledge, then I will take the better action and make amends for my earlier promise."

When deception advances Islam, the deception is not a sin.

B5,59,369 Mohammed asked, "Who will kill Ka'b, the enemy of Allah and Mohammed?"

Bin Maslama rose and responded, "O Mohammed! Would it please you if I killed him?"

Mohammed answered, "Yes."

Bin Maslama then said, "Give me permission to deceive him with lies so that my plot will succeed."

Mohammed replied, "You may speak falsely to him."

Ali was raised by Mohammed from the age of ten and became the fourth caliph. Ali pronounced the following on lies and deception.

B9,84,64 When I relate to you the words of Mohammed, by Allah, I would rather die than bear false witness to his teachings. However, if I should say something unrelated to the prophet, then it might very well be a lie so that I might deceive my enemy. Without question, I heard Mohammed say, "In the final days before Redemption there will emerge groups of foolish youths who will say all the right things but their faith will go no further than their mouths and will flee from their religion like an arrow. So, kill the apostates wherever you find them, because whoever does so will be rewarded on Judgment Day."

Deceit is part of Islamic war against the Kafirs.

B4,52,267 Mohammed: "The king of Persia will be destroyed, and no one shall assume his throne. Caesar will certainly be destroyed and no Caesar will follow him; his coffers will be spent in Allah's cause." Mohammed cried out, "Jihad is deceit."

Deceit in war:

M032,6303 According to Mohammed, someone who strives to promote harmony amongst the faithful and says or conveys good things is not a liar. Ibn Shihab said that he had heard only three exceptions to the rules governing false statements: lies are permissible in war, to reconcile differences between the faithful, and to reconcile a husband and wife through the manipulation or twisting of words.

The name for deception that advances Islam is taqiyya *(safeguard, concealment, piety). But a Muslim must never lie to another Muslim. A lie should never be told unless there is no other way to accomplish the task Al Tabarani, in Al Awsat, said, "Lies are sins except when they are told for the welfare of a Muslim or for saving him from a disaster."* [1]

Another example of sacred deceit, taqiyya:

I224 A member of the Abyssinian royalty, called the Negus, became convinced of the truth of Islam. He was accused by the Christians of leaving his religion. The Negus wrote on a piece of paper, "There is no god but Allah and Mohammed is his prophet. Jesus was a Muslim, born of Mary, conceived without a father." He the then pinned the statement under his shirt over his heart. [These are classical Islamic statements.] When the other Abyssinians accused the Negus of leaving Christianity and they said, "Jesus was the Son of God." The Negus placed his hand over his heart (and the paper with the statement) and told the Christians, "I testify that Jesus was no more than this." The Christians took him at his word and left him. When Mohammed heard this, he prayed for the Negus when he died.

---

1. Bat Ye'or, *The Dhimmi* (Cranbury, N.J.: Associated University Presses, 2003), 392.

LAW

The hadiths are the basis of the Sharia, Islamic law. Here is a hadith about capital crimes. Killing a Kafir is not a capital crime.

B1,3,111 I [Abu] asked Ali, "Do you know of any sources of law that were revealed to Mohammed other than the Koran?" Ali responded, "None except for Allah's law, or the ability of reason given by Allah to a Muslim, or these written precepts I possess." I said, "What are these written rules?" Ali answered, "They concern the blood money paid by a killer to a victim's relatives, the method of ransoming a captive's release from the enemy, and the law that a Muslim must never be killed as punishment for killing a Kafir."

If a father converts to Islam and his child or wife does not, then he or she cannot be an heir.

B8,80,756 Mohammed: "A Muslim cannot be the heir of a Kafir and a Muslim cannot have a Kafir as an heir."

TREATMENT OF FELLOW MUSLIMS

Do not harm another Muslim.

B1,2,9 Mohammed: "The difference between a Muslim and an Immigrant[1] is that a Muslim avoids harming other Muslims with words or deeds, while an Immigrant merely abandons everything that Allah forbids."

Weapons in the mosque are acceptable. The mosque is a political center as well as a community center and a place of worship.

B1,8,443 Mohammed: "Arrows should be held by their heads when carried through mosques or markets so that they do not harm a Muslim."

B9,88,193 Mohammed: "You should not aim your weapons at other Muslims; you never know, Satan might tempt you to harm them, and your sin would send you to Hell."

Killing a Muslim is a crime.

B5,58,194 I asked Ibn Abbas about these two verses from the Koran:

> 25:68 *They do not call upon other gods along with Allah and do not kill those whom Allah has forbidden to be killed [other Muslims] except for just cause.*

> 4:93 *For those who intentionally kill another Muslim, Hell will be their punishment, where they will live forever. The wrath of Allah*

---

1. Mohammed emigrated from Mecca to Medina. The Immigrant is a sacred figure in Islam.

will be upon them, He will curse them, and they will receive terrible torture.

He said, "When the verse from sura 25 was revealed to Mohammed, the pagans in Mecca wondered about their chances at salvation and said, 'We have taken lives that Allah has declared sacred. We have worshiped other gods alongside Allah, and we are guilty of fornication.' Allah then revealed to Mohammed:

> 25:70 *Allah is forgiving and merciful, and whoever repents and does good has truly turned to Allah with an acceptable and true conversion.*

This verse then dealt with the pagans from Mecca.

> 4:93 *For those who intentionally kill another Muslim, Hell will be their punishment, where they will live forever. The wrath of Allah will be upon them, He will curse them, and they will receive terrible torture.*

This verse means that if a man murders another, despite a full understanding of Islam and its laws and requirements, then he shall be punished by burning in Hell forever.

I then mentioned this to Mujahid who elaborated by saying, 'The man who regrets his crime is excepted.'"

In business, a Muslim should never cheat a Muslim.

B9,86,109 Mohammed said, "A neighbor has a greater expectation of help from his neighbor[2] than anyone else." Some said, "If a man wants to buy a house there is no harm done if he uses trickery to prevent another from buying it." Abu Abdullah said, "So that man says that some people are allowed to play tricks on other Muslims though Mohammed said, 'When doing business with other Muslims do not sell them sick animals or defective or stolen goods.' "

B8,73,70 Mohammed: "Harming a Muslim is an evil act; killing a Muslim means rejecting Allah."

A Muslim can swear a false oath by any other god and not be accountable.

B8,73,73 Mohammed: "A Muslim who swears a false oath by the god of another religion is not obligated to fulfill that promise because he cannot be bound by a faith he does not hold."

---

2. Other hadiths show that neighbor meant other Muslims who lived in their own neighborhoods.

POSITION TOWARD OTHER RELIGIONS

Well before Mohammed, since the most ancient days, Mecca had been a center of religious tolerance. Many religions used Mecca as a pilgrim site. The Kabah was a temple of every known religion, including Christianity. This Sunna occurred after Mohammed conquered Mecca.

B1,8,365 On the Day of Nahr, Abu Bakr dispatched Ali and others to Mecca to make a public declaration: "After this year no Kafir may make a pilgrimage to Mecca to worship, and the ancient rituals performed around the Kabah are now forbidden."

Mohammed's deathbed wishes were to create religious apartheid in Arabia and to use money to influence Kafirs for Islam.

B4,52,288 Ibn Abbas said, "Thursday, what a momentous thing happened on Thursday!" He then wept until his tears muddied the earth. Then he said, "On Thursday, Mohammed's condition worsened and he [Mohammed] said, 'Bring me a scribe with his tools so that I may leave you instructions that will keep you from going astray.' Those present disagreed with one another, something one should not do in the presence of a prophet. They said, 'Mohammed is gravely ill.' Mohammed said, 'Leave me alone; my condition now is better than what you wish for me.'

"On his deathbed Mohammed gave three final orders saying, 'First, drive the Kafirs from Arabia. Second, give gifts and show respect to foreign officials as I have done.' I forgot the third command."

RESPECT

B1,2,45 Mohammed: "A Muslim acting sincerely and hoping to gain Allah's pleasure who joins the funeral party of a fellow Muslim and remains to the end of the service will be rewarded with two Qirats,[1] each the size of a mountain. The Muslim who offers the funeral prayer but does not stay for the burial will be rewarded one Qirat."

SECURITY

B1,8,386 Mohammed: "Whoever follows our prayer rituals and dietary commands is a Muslim and is protected by Allah and Mohammed. Do not betray those protected by Allah because, if you do, you also betray Allah."

This hadith details security, education, and slavery.

B4,53,397 Ali: "Muslims have no need to read anything other than the word of Allah and the legal regulations in this paper that govern the

---

1. The meaning of this term is unclear.

compensation for injuries, the condition of livestock used to pay taxes that support the needy, the payment of blood money, and the status of Medina as a sanctuary. Therefore, anyone who sins against the doctrine, or falsely adds to it, or protects someone who does will be cursed by Allah, the people, and the angels. No amount of good acts will mitigate this transgression. Any freed slave who rejects the mastery of his former owner for the friendship of another will also be cursed. Protection granted by one Muslim must be upheld by all Muslims. Whoever violates the protection granted by a Muslim will also be cursed by Allah, the people, and the angels."

SLAVERY

The reason for the tax exemption on horses was jihad. Mohammed gave cavalrymen three times the amount he gave foot soldiers from the spoils of war (the wealth of the vanquished) to build a better cavalry.

B2,24,542 Mohammed: "Horses and slaves owned by a Muslim are tax exempt."

It is forbidden to capture a Muslim and make him a slave. If a slave converts to Islam, then there is a benefit in freeing him. But there is no benefit in freeing a Kafir slave. Islamic slavery is a blessing because sooner or later the slave or the slave's descendants will convert to Islam in order to be free.

B3,46,693 Mohammed said, "If a man frees a Muslim slave, Allah will free him from the fires of Hell in the same way that he freed the slave." Bin Marjana said that, after he related that revelation to Ali, the man freed a slave for whom he had been offered one thousand dinars by Abdullah.

THEFT

B8,81,793 When Ubada and a group of others pledged allegiance to Mohammed, the prophet said, "I accept your oath that you will worship only Allah and that you will not steal, kill unwanted children, slander others by lying or gossiping, or disobey my moral commands. If you honor all these promises, you will be rewarded by Allah in the afterlife. If you break any of these promises and are legally punished, you have made atonement and need not fear the punishment of Allah. However, if the will of Allah shields your sins from the eyes of man, your fate is in His hands to punish or forgive as he sees fit."

Abu Abdullah said, "If a thief repents after his hand is severed, his testimony will be accepted. Any Muslim who repents after punishment will have his testimony accepted."

B8,81,783 Aisha: "While Mohammed was alive, a thief's hand was only severed if he stole something as valuable as a shield."

B8,81,791 Mohammed: "Allah curses a thief, whether he steals an egg, a helmet, or a rope. Thieves are punished by cutting off their hands."

ETHICS OF KILLING WOMEN AND CHILDREN IN JIHAD

Killing children in jihad is acceptable. But in other hadiths we find they should not be killed. Both moral positions are Sunna; so both positions are available.

M019,4322 When Mohammed was told that Muslims had killed the children of their enemies during raids, Mohammed said that it was permissible because "they are from them."

But here we find that only certain children should be killed.

M019,4457 Yazid B. Hurmus said that Mohammed disapproved of killing children and believed that Muslims should not kill them unless they could tell the difference between a prospective Muslim and a prospective Kafir. In which case, it was permissible to kill the prospective Kafir child and allow the potential Muslim child to live.

Here are two examples that determine the rules of jihad. They contradict each other, so the resolution is that either can be used as needed.

M019,4319 In one of Mohammed's battles, it was discovered that a woman had been killed by the Muslims; however, he did not approve of killing women and children.

M019,4321 According to Sa'b B. Jaththama, Mohammed said, "They are from them," when told of the killing of women and children by Muslims during a raid.

This is the Sunna of Mohammed

JIHAD

CHAPTER 2

*61:11 Believe in Allah and His messenger and fight valiantly
for Allah's cause [jihad] with both your wealth and your
lives. It would be better for you, if you only knew it!*

The ethical system of the Hadith prepares the foundation of jihad. There is one set of ethics for the Muslim and another set of ethics for the Kafir. There are two ways to deal with Kafirs. One is to treat them as inferiors but in a kindly way. The other is jihad. About 21% of Bukhari is about jihad.

Jihad is a unique word. Its actual meaning is struggle or effort. Islam talks of two kinds—the lesser jihad and the greater jihad. The greater jihad is spiritual effort or internal struggle, to stop smoking, for example, or control one's greed. However, the term "lesser jihad" never occurs in any authoritative hadith. There are about 2% of the hadiths in Bukhari that hold up other things as equal to jihad. The other 98% of the jihad hadiths refer to armed violence. It was violence that gave Islam its success and that is why nearly every jihad hadith calls armed jihad the best action a Muslim can perform.

Jihad, armed struggle, is usually called "holy war," but this term is simplistic and far too narrow. It means, in fact, fighting in the cause of Allah, and it encompasses an entire way of life.

The dual ethics established by the sacred texts of Islam—treating Muslims one way and Kafirs another—are the basis of jihad. Perhaps the clearest expression of this duality is a phrase known to all Muslims: The world is divided into—

dar al Islam, land of submission, and

dar al harb, land of war.

The land of war is the country that is free of Islam, free of Allah. The land of the Kafir must become the land of those who have submitted and are the slaves of Allah. The Trilogy repeatedly stresses that Islam should be in a state of constant pressure against Kafirs; therefore, the relation between Islam and the rest of the world is sacred war or temporary peace. This struggle is eternal, universal, and obligatory for the

Muslim community. The only pause in jihad comes through the need for Islam to strengthen itself. Peace is temporary. War is permanent.

Jihad is laid out in all three of the Trilogy texts.

THE KORAN OF MECCA AND MEDINA

The early portions of the Koran were written in Mecca and are generally religious in nature. The part of the Koran written in Medina is very different. Islam developed a complete political ideology there. The Koran of Medina lays out the divine right of aggression and violence in all forms against the Kafir.

The Koran has 111 verses devoted to jihad. Three chapters of the Koran are titled War Treasure, Battle Array, Victory and War Steeds. Nearly all of the jihadic verses are found in the Koran of Medina. Since the jihadic verses were written later than the "peaceful" ones of Mecca, the jihadic verses can abrogate or nullify the peaceful ones.

Below we have examples of the dual nature of political Islam. These following verses do not contradict each other; they merely express the dual nature of the Islamic ethical system. They are equally acceptable and used according to the given situation.

KORAN OF MECCA

73:10 *Listen to what they [Kafirs] say with patience and leave them with dignity.*

109:6 *To you be your religion, and to me my religion.*

20:130 *So be patient with what they say, and constantly celebrate your Lord's praise before the sun rises and before it sets and for part of the night and at both ends of the day so that you may please Him.*

50:45 *We know exactly what the Kafirs say, and you should not compel them. Use the Koran to warn those who fear my threat.*

10:99 *But if the Lord had pleased, all men on earth would have believed together. Would you compel men to become believers?*

45:14 *Tell the believers to forgive those who do not hope for the days of Allah. It is up to Him to reward men according to their actions.*

43:88 *And the Prophet will cry, "My Lord, truly these are people who do not believe." So turn away from them and say, "Peace." They will soon find out.*

KORAN OF MEDINA

2:191 *Kill them wherever you find them, and drive them out of whatever place from which they have driven you, which is worse than murder.*

9:123 *Believers, fight the Kafirs who are near you, and let them find you to be tough and hard.*

8:12 *Then your Lord spoke to His angels and said, "I will be with you. Give strength to the believers. I will send terror into the Kafirs' hearts, cut off their heads and even the tips of their fingers!"*

9:29 *Make war on those who have received the Scriptures [Jews and Christians] but do not believe in Allah or in the Last Day. They do not forbid what Allah and His Messenger have forbidden. The Christians and Jews do not follow the religion of truth until they submit and pay the poll tax [jizya] and they are humiliated.*

2:193 *Fight them until you are no longer persecuted and the religion of Allah reigns absolute, but if they give up, then only fight the evil-doers.*

5:33 *The only reward for those who war against Allah and His messengers and strive to commit mischief on the earth is that they will be slain or crucified, have their alternate hands and feet cut off, or be banished from the land.*

47:4 *When you encounter the Kafirs on the battlefield, cut off their heads until you have thoroughly defeated them and then take the prisoners and tie them up firmly.*

THE SIRA

The ideology of political Islam is laid out in the Sira, the life of Mohammed, and the Koran gives the divine vision, similar to a political constitution. In Mecca, aggression was limited to persuasion, arguments, threats, and fist fights. Mohammed tried these methods for thirteen years and gathered 150 followers. In Medina, he used war and conquest to rule all of Arabia.

Roughly seventy-five percent of the material of Mohammed's biography is devoted to jihad. In Medina, over a nine-year period, Mohammed personally attended twenty-seven raids. There are thirty-eight other battles and expeditions in his biography. This is a total of sixty-five armed events[1], not including assassinations and executions, for an average of

1. A. Guillaume, *The Life of Muhammad* [the sira], (Karachi: Oxford University Press, 1967) 659-60.

one every seven weeks over a period of nine years. This aggression enabled Mohammed to triumph over all of the ancient Arabic religions and political centers and rule Arabia as its first king.

JIHAD IN THE HADITH

The Hadith spells out the details of jihad. Who can be killed, under what circumstances, at what times, the actual words to be said upon attack, how to handle defeat, what to do with prisoners, how to build morale, and more are drawn from the ideal words and actions of Mohammed. The Hadith is a precise tactical manual for jihad.

The hadiths call armed struggle "fighting in Allah's Cause" or "Allah's Cause." Many of the hadiths focus on jihad.

SUMMARY

The Koran gives the divine authorization for political Islam and jihad.
The Sira shows the strategy of conquest.
The Hadith is the tactical manual.

THE FUNDAMENTALS OF JIHAD

This hadith summarizes all the key elements of jihad. (Only the fourth item, the Day of Resurrection, is purely religious in nature). It tells us that the whole world must submit to Islam; Kafirs are the enemy simply by not being Muslims. To achieve this dominance Islam may use terror and violence. It may use psychological warfare, fear, theft. It may take the spoils of war from Kafirs. Violence and terror are made sacred by the Koran. Peace comes only with submission to Islam.

B1,7,331 Mohammed:
I have been given five things which were not given to any one else before me:

1. Allah made me *victorious by awe, by His frightening my enemies* for a distance of one month's journey.

2. *The earth has been made for me and for my followers,* a place for praying and a place to perform rituals; therefore, anyone of my followers can pray wherever the time of a prayer is due.

3. *The spoils of war has been made lawful for me* yet it was not lawful for anyone else before me.

4. I have been given the right of intercession on the Day of Resurrection.

5. Every Prophet used to be sent to his nation only but *I have been sent to all mankind.* [Emphasis added.]

Political Islam is universal and eternal.

M001,0031 Mohammed: "I have been ordered to wage war against mankind until they accept that there is no god but Allah and that they believe I am His prophet and accept all revelations spoken through me. When they do these things I will protect their lives and property unless otherwise justified by Islamic law, in which case their fate lies in Allah's hands."

OBLIGATION

All Muslims have an obligation to perform jihad. Jihad is second only to prayer and respect for one's parents.

B1,10,505 Abdullah asked Mohammed, "What act is most beloved by Allah?" Mohammed answered, "To pray at the specified times." Abdullah then asked, "What is the next highest good?" He said, "Honor and obey your parents." I asked a third time, "What is the next highest good?" Mohammed replied, "To wage holy war in the name of Allah." Abdullah concluded, "I did not ask the next highest good, but if I had, Mohammed would have told me."

Jihad is one of the best actions that a Muslim can perform.

B2,26,594 Someone asked Mohammed, "What is the greatest act a Muslim can perform?" He said, "Accept Allah as the only god and that I am His prophet." Mohammed was then asked, "What is the next best act?" He answered, "To wage holy war in the name of Allah." Mohammed was then asked, "What is the next highest good?" He replied, "To make the sacred pilgrimage."

The following hadith is one of the few references about the greater jihad (spiritual effort). Only about three percent of the hadiths concerning jihad are about the greater jihad, spiritual struggle. The other ninety-seven percent are about jihad as supreme war.

B2,26,595 One of Mohammed's wives, Aisha, declared to him, "We believe fighting holy war is the most righteous action for Muslims." He replied, "Women can best wage jihad by taking the holy pilgrimages." Aisha persisted, "Should not women fight alongside men during jihad?" Mohammed responded, "The best way for women to fight for Islam is by doing what is acceptable to Allah, which is for them to partake in holy pilgrimage." Aisha assented and said, "After that conversation with Mohammed, I resolved to never forgo [pilgrimage to Mecca]."

To commit suicide is a sure path to Hell. But to kill oneself in jihad is a sure path to eternal pleasure in Paradise.

B5,59,509 The army was arranged in rows at the battle at Khaybar. Amir's sword was short, and he aimed at the knee of a Jew. The sharp blade glanced off the Jew's knee and cut Amir's leg. He bled to death. After the battle, Al Akwa was sad and Mohammed asked him, "What is bothering you?" Al Akwa said, "They say Amir is lost because he killed himself." Mohammed said, "No, they are wrong. Amir will get a double reward [an elevated place in Paradise]." Mohammed raised two fingers. "Amir was a strong fighter in the Cause of Allah. There are few who have achieved such goodness as Amir."

Killing yourself in jihad is good, but suicide is a great sin.

B8,73 Mohammed: "If someone kills himself, by any means in this world, then he will be tortured on the Day of Resurrection in the same manner."

The best Muslim is a jihadist. A saintly man is second best.

M020,4655 Mohammed: "The Muslim who lives the best life is the man who is always prepared to wage holy war in the name of Allah and who is constantly alert for the sound of war or a cry for help and always willing to face certain death. The next most virtuous life for a Muslim is the hermit who abides on a mountain or valley tending his herd, praying regularly, giving zakat [charity tax to be spent on Muslims], and worshiping Allah until he dies. There are no better men than these."

To avoid jihad is a great sin. The jihadist must be unafraid of death and never retreat except as a strategy. The enemy, the Kafir, must never be given mercy.

B4,51,28: Mohammed commanded, "Shun the seven deadly sins." Asked to elaborate, Mohammed said, "Worshiping gods other than Allah, witchcraft, the unsanctified murder of a believer, lending money at excessive rates of interest, squandering the assets of a ward or orphan, granting mercy to or fleeing from an unbelieving enemy in battle, and impugning the character of true believing, pure, and virginal women."

To be a real Muslim, one must aspire to be a jihadist.

M020,4696 Mohammed: "The man who dies without participating in jihad, who never desired to wage holy war, dies the death of a hypocrite."

Here we have prophetic hadiths. Jihad will be practiced into the future.

B4,152,146 Mohammed: "A time will come when the people will wage holy war, and it will be asked, 'Is there any amongst you who has enjoyed the company of Mohammed?' They will say: 'Yes.' And then victory will be bestowed upon them. They will wage holy war again, and it will be asked: 'Is there any among you who has enjoyed the company of the companions of Mohammed?' They will say: 'Yes.' And then victory will be bestowed on them."

M020,4712 Mohammed: "You shall conquer many lands and Allah will grant you victory over your enemies in battle, but none of you should stop practicing for war."

Fighting in jihad is demanded for all Muslims except for the frail or the cripple. To sit at home is inferior to jihad. Jihad is an obligation for all times and all places and for all Muslims.

B6,60,118 After the following verse was revealed to Mohammed, he called for a scribe,

> *"Not equal are those believers who sit at home and those who strive and fight in the Cause of Allah."*

After the scribe arrived with his writing utensils, Mohammed dictated his revelation. Ibn Um Maktum, who was present, exclaimed, "O Mohammed! But I am blind." A new revelation was then revealed that said:

> 4:95 *Believers who stay at home in safety, other than those who are disabled, are not equal to those who fight with their wealth and their lives for Allah's cause [jihad].*

Muslims should dedicate their jihad to their parents.

B8,73,3 A man once asked Mohammed, "Should I join the holy war?" Mohammed responded by asking if the man's parents were alive. When the man affirmed that they were, Mohammed answered, "Join the struggle for their sake."

Jihad is one of the highest goals of Islam, equal to charity and prayer.

B8,73,35 Mohammed: "The Muslim who does charitable works for the poor or elderly is like a holy warrior or a devout person who fasts all day and prays all night."

When the leader calls for jihad, every Muslim should take part immediately.

B4,52,42 Mohammed: "After the conquest of Mecca, there is no need to migrate to Medina, but holy war and the willingness to participate still remain. If your ruler demands warriors, answer his call immediately."

Jihad is the best deed. The smallest action in jihad is rewarded more than prayer and fasting.

B4,52,44 A man said to Mohammed, "Tell me what act is rewarded as much as jihad." Mohammed replied, "I do not know of any." The prophet added, "Can a Muslim warrior, while in the field of battle, perform his prayers according to ritual or fast without stopping?" The man said, "No one can do that." Abu-Huraira then added, "The Muslim jihadi is rewarded by Allah merely for the footsteps of his mount while it is tethered and grazing."

An ordinary jihadist is superior to a saint.

B4,52,45 Someone asked, "Mohammed, who is the best person?" Mohammed said, "A Muslim who uses all of his strength and resources striving in Allah's cause." The person then asked, "Who is the next best person?" Mohammed replied, "A Muslim who remains secluded from the world, praying to Allah and not bothering the people with foolishness."

Here is Allah's contract with all Islam: to die in jihad is the sure way to go to Paradise. If the jihadist does not die, then he can keep what wealth he takes with violence from the enemy, the Kafir.

B4,52,46 Mohammed: "A Muslim holy warrior, fighting for Allah's cause is like a person who does nothing but fast and pray. Allah promises that anyone killed while fighting for His cause will be admitted without question into Paradise. If such a holy warrior survives the battles, he can return home with the captured property and possessions of the defeated."

A jihadist fights so that Islam will triumph, not just for wealth or fame. The jihadist is the purest and best Muslim.

B4,52,65 A man asked Mohammed, "One man fights for wealth, one man fights to achieve fame, and another fights for pride. Who among them fights for the cause of Allah?" Mohammed said, "The man who fights so that Islam should dominate is the man who fights for Allah's cause."

B4,52,72 Mohammed: "After entering Paradise no one would want to return to the world even though he might have everything in it, the only exception being the Muslim warrior who would return to be martyred ten times more for the honor he received from Allah."

All the Kafirs who fight against jihad are doomed to burn in Hell for defending their culture and civilization.

B4,52,72 Mohammed told us that Allah revealed to him that "any holy warrior killed will go to Paradise." Umar asked the prophet, "Is it true that Muslims killed in battle will go to Paradise and Kafirs who are killed in battle will go to Hell?" Mohammed said, "Yes."

A Muslim should support jihadists in every way. This includes financing the fighters and supporting their families.

B4,52,96 Mohammed: "Anyone who arms a jihadist is rewarded just as a fighter would be; anyone who gives proper care to a holy warrior's dependents is rewarded just as a fighter would be."

The smallest detail of supporting jihad brings a great reward.

B4,52,105 Mohammed: "If a man, motivated by belief in Allah and the promises Allah makes, gives a horse to be used for jihad, he will be rewarded on Judgment Day for the food and water the horse consumed and the waste it expelled."

Practicing jihad for even one day puts a believer in Paradise and is better than all the world.

B4,52,142 Mohammed: "To battle Kafirs in jihad for even one day is greater than the entire earth and everything on it. A spot in Paradise smaller than your riding crop is greater than the entire earth and everything on it. A day or a night's travel in jihad is greater than the entire world and everything on it."

M020,4645 Mohammed said: "Abu Sa'id, anybody that happily acclaims Allah as his God, Islam as his faith, and Mohammed as his prophet must be admitted into Paradise." Abu Sa'id marveled at this and said, "Mohammed, say that again." Mohammed repeated his statement and added, "Another act raises a man's status in Paradise a hundred-fold; the difference between one level and another is equivalent to the distance between the heavens and the earth." Abu Sa'id asked, "What is this act?" Mohammed said, "Wage war for Allah! Wage war for Allah!"

Jihad cannot stop until all of the world has submitted to Islam. All Kafirs' lives and wealth can and will be taken by jihad. Only those who submit to Islam will be spared.

B4,52,196 Mohammed: "I have been directed to fight the Kafir until every one of them admits, 'There is only one god and that is Allah.' Whoever says, 'There is only one god and that is Allah,' his body and possessions will be protected by me except for violations of Islamic law, in which case his fate is with Allah, to be punished or forgiven, as He sees fit."

One of the first things Mohammed taught new Muslims was the distribution of the spoils of war.

B4,53,327 A delegation came to Mohammed from Rabi'a and asked the prophet for instructions for their tribe. Mohammed said, "I command you to perform five actions and I forbid you to do one act: accept Allah as the only god, perform your prayers strictly according to ritual, pay the charitable tax [*zakat*] for the support of the needy, fast during the month of Ramadan, give twenty percent of the property looted from Kafirs to Allah, and never drink alcohol."

INVESTMENT OF MONEY IN JIHAD

The very best use of money is to spend it on jihad. Mohammed was the perfect example because he was indifferent to the personal use of money. He spent almost nothing on his household but gave generously to jihad.

B2,24,489 I [Al-Ahnaf] was with members of the Quraysh tribe when a disheveled man approached and said, "Tell the hoarders of material wealth that they will forever suffer painful torture in the fires of Hell." After speaking, the rough-looking man, whom I did not recognize, walked a short distance away and sat down. I joined him and said, "The people did not like what you said." He replied, "Those people don't know anything. My friend told me that it is so." I asked him his friend's name. He said, "Mohammed asked me, 'Do you see Mount Uhud?' I said, 'Yes,' and I looked to the sun to gauge the time of day because I believed that he wished me to perform a task for him. Mohammed said, 'If I had a pile of gold as big as Mount Uhud, I would spend it all but three dinars on jihad.' Those people do not understand Islam, so they hoard material wealth. No, by Allah, so long as I am alive, I won't need their material wealth or their advice on religion."

Allah rewards those who give to jihad and curses those who do not.

B2,24,522 Mohammed: "Two angels descend from Paradise each day. One says, 'O, Allah! Reward those who contribute to jihad,' and the other says, 'O, Allah! Kill those who refuse to support jihad.'"

Jihad is supported by the Islamic tax structure and can make a man rich.

B2,24,547 A man ordered by Mohammed to collect a duty supporting jihad returned to him and reported that Ibn Jamil, Khalid, and Abbas refused to pay the tax. Mohammed asked, "Ibn Jamil was a poor man made rich by Allah and me. What makes him think he can refuse to pay his tax? It is unfair to ask Khalid to pay the tax because he remains a holy warrior for Allah. Abbas, however, is my uncle and the tax is mandatory for him. In fact, he should pay twice the amount."

Allah says a Muslim should spend his money on jihad.

B6,60,41 Hudhaifa said, "The following verse was revealed to Mohammed regarding the financial support of jihad."

> 2:195 *Spend your wealth generously for Allah's cause [jihad] and do not use your own hands to contribute to your destruction. Do good, for surely Allah loves those that do good.*

B8,78,633 I [Abu Dhar] joined Mohammed as he was sitting in the shade of the Kabah. He kept repeating, "They are the losers, by Allah! They are the losers!" I fretted to myself, "What have I done wrong? Does he perceive something improper in me?" As I sat beside him, Mohammed kept repeating, "They are the losers." Allah knows how anxious I was. I could not remain silent. I asked him, "Who are the losers? I would sacrifice my parents for you, Mohammed." He said, "The losers are the rich, except those who give money for jihad."

B4,52,94 Mohammed said, "Whoever spends even a small amount on jihad will be welcomed by name by the gate-keepers of Paradise."

Abu Bakr said, "O, Mohammed! People like that will never be destroyed."

Mohammed said, "It is my wish that you will be such a person."

M020,4668 Mohammed: "A person who financially supports a fighter for jihad is morally equivalent to an actual fighter. A person who cares for a warrior's family during his service is morally equivalent to an actual fighter."

The wealth of Islam comes from jihad.

B4,53,350 Mohammed: "When the Persian king is destroyed, his line will end with him. When Caesar is destroyed, there will be no more Caesars. By Him who holds my life in His hands, you will spend his wealth in jihad against the rest of the world."

GOALS

The goal of jihad is the dominance of Islam over all other political systems and religions.

B1,3,125 A man asked Mohammed, "Mohammed, what manner of fighting can be considered done for the sake of Allah? Some fight because they are angry and some for their pride." Mohammed looked up at the man and said, "The man who fights to make Islam dominant is the man who fights for Allah's cause."

All other religions must submit to Islam. Then and only then will jihad stop. Until that time no person, other than a Muslim, is safe.

B1,8,387 Mohammed said, "I have been commanded to fight the Kafirs until they admit: 'There is one god and He is Allah.' If they admit this, pray as we do, face Mecca as we do, and prepare their meat as we do, then their persons and possessions will be sacred to us and we will not limit them except in legal matters. Their judgment rests with Allah."

"Abu Hamza, what makes a person's life or possessions sacred?"

He [Abu Hamza] answered, "If a person gives witness that there is but one god, Allah, and if he prays like we do and faces Mecca, and if he obeys our dietary commands, then he is a Muslim and has the same entitlements and obligations as the rest of us. These things make a person's body and possessions sacred."

When jihad is successful, it is not the Muslim who is successful but Allah. Jihad is the triumph of Allah over the Kafir.

B3,27,23 Whenever Mohammed returned from a Holy Battle, or pilgrimage, he used to say, "Allah is great," three times. Every time Mohammed returned from jihad or Hajj, he would exclaim at every hill three times, "God is great," and then he would say, "There is no god but Allah; He is perfect and has no partners. He reigns over all kingdoms and all praise is due him. He is all-powerful. We return filled with repentance: praying, bowing down, and giving praise. Allah honored His promise and gave victory to His slave. Allah alone subjugated the Kafirs."

REWARDS

A Muslim martyr is one who kills for Allah and Islam. But his killing must be pure and devoted only to Allah. If his motivation is pure, then the jihadist will achieve Paradise or be able to take the wealth of the Kafir.

B1,2,35 Mohammed said, "The man who joins jihad, compelled by nothing except sincere belief in Allah and His Prophets, and survives, will be rewarded by Allah either in the afterlife or with the spoils of war. If he is killed in battle and dies a martyr, he will be admitted into Paradise. Were it not for the difficulties it would cause my followers, I would never stay behind while my soldiers head off for jihad. If I could, I would love to be martyred in jihad, be resurrected, and martyred again and again for Allah."

One of Mohammed's instructions for new converts was to share the wealth taken in jihad: one-fifth had to be given to Islam. In addition, the new Muslim had to pay a tax to Islam.

B1,10,501 Leaders from an Arab tribe came to Mohammed and said, "Our tribe is separated from you by distance and enemies, and we can only visit during the sacred months. Give us commandments so that we may bring them to our people." Mohammed said, "I command you to do four things, and I forbid you to do one. The things you must do are admit that there is but one god, Allah, and Mohammed is His prophet, strictly follow rules governing prayer, pay taxes to support the needy, and finally give me one-fifth of all spoils of war. The thing that you must not do is drink alcohol."

No matter what sins a jihadist commits, he will not go to Hell.

B2,13,30 I [Abu Abs] heard Mohammed say, "Anyone who even gets his feet dirty performing jihad will be saved from Hell by Allah."

The pure jihadist must commit his life and wealth to jihad. If he can reach this highest form of devotion, then not even the pilgrimage to Mecca (the Hajj) can surpass it.

B2,15,86 Mohammed said, "No good act during the rest of the year is better than departing on Hajj." Some of his companions asked, "What about jihad?" Mohammed answered, "Even jihad is inferior unless a man knowingly risks and loses both life and property for the sake of Allah."

M020,4649 Mohammed: "Except debt, all sins of a martyr are forgiven."

B3,27,6 I [Qatada] questioned Anas about the number of times Mohammed made the lesser pilgrimage. He answered, "Four." Once he even distributed spoils of war amongst the people. I assumed he meant the spoils from the battle of Hunain. I asked how many times he made the greater pilgrimage to Mecca. Anas responded, "Once."

B3,31,121 Mohammed said, "Anyone who gives more than his share to support the cost of jihad will be called and greeted at the gates of Paradise with, 'O slave of Allah! Here is wealth.' Anyone who scrupulously prayed will be called into Paradise from the gate of prayer; anyone who joined jihad will be called from the gate of jihad; anyone who fasted correctly will be called to the gate of fulfillment; anyone who gave alms will be called from the gate of charity." Abu Bakr said, "I would sacrifice my parents for you Mohammed! Nothing bad will happen to those called from those gates. Will anyone be called from all of them?" Mohammed answered, "Yes, I hope that you are one."

Paradise lies in the shade of swords.

M020,4681 Mohammed said, "Certainly, the gates of Paradise lie in the shade of swords." A shabby man rose and asked Abu Musa if he had heard Mohammed say this. "Yes," he replied. The shabby man then rejoined his friends and said his good-byes. He then unsheathed his sword, broke and discarded its scabbard, advanced upon the enemy, and fought until he was killed.

M020,4694 Mohammed: "A man who sincerely pursues martyrdom, even if he is not killed, shall still receive its reward."

B3,34,294 Jihadists were given mixed dates captured as spoils of war and would often exchange twelve pounds of mixed dates for six pounds of good dates. Mohammed discouraged this as he believed it to be a form of usury.

After jihad, Ali had the money necessary for the obligatory marriage dowry.

B3,34,302 As my [Ali's] share of the spoils of war I received an old she-camel, and Mohammed gave me another from his share. When my marriage to Fatima [Mohammed's daughter] approached, I hired a Jewish goldsmith to assist me in bringing a load of ldhkhir grass for resale to other goldsmiths, the proceeds to pay for my wedding reception.

A jihadist can benefit Islam and achieve personal gain.

B3,34,313 We departed with Mohammed in the year of the battle of Hunain. Mohammed gave me a captured suit of armor which I sold. I [Abu Qatada] took the money from the armor and bought a garden near the Bani Salama tribe. That was the first property I received after converting to Islam.

Mohammed became rich from jihad, so rich that he could pay the debts of dead jihadists.

B3,37,495 Every time a Muslim died in debt and was brought to Mohammed he asked, "Has he any property to repay his debts?" If the dead man had assets, then Mohammed would offer the funeral prayers. If not, he told the man's friends to offer the funeral prayer. After Allah made Mohammed rich by conquering the Kafirs, he said, "I have a greater obligation than other Muslims to be the guardian of Islam; therefore if a Muslim dies in debt, I am responsible for settling that debt. If a Muslim dies leaving assets and no debt, then it will belong to his heirs."

B3,39,527 Umar [the second caliph]: "If not for the sake of later generations, I would have divided the land I conquered among my soldiers as Mohammed did the land of Khaybar."

B3,40,563 As my share of spoils of war from the battle of Badr I [Ali] received a she-camel, and Mohammed gave me another. I allowed them to rest outside the door of one of the Helpers. My plan was to use the camels to haul Idhkhir grass to market. The price I received for the Idhkhir grass would pay for the banquet following my upcoming wedding with Fatima. A Jewish goldsmith who was to accompany me on the enterprise was with me.

Hamza was in a Helper's house drinking wine when a female singer urged him to slaughter the she-camels and cook them for the guests. So Hamza grabbed his sword, killed both camels, and began to butcher them. When I saw this, I went to Mohammed and told him what Hamza had done. Mohammed, accompanied by Zaid and me, went to Hamza and scolded him. Hamza looked at us and said, "Aren't you the slaves of my ancestors?" Mohammed backed out of the house and left. This was before the ban on drinking alcohol.

B3,44,668 I [Abaya] heard my grandfather say, "We were traveling with Mohammed and the people captured some camels and sheep from Kafirs. The people were hungry, and so they quickly slaughtered the beasts and began to cook them in pots. Mohammed was in the rear of the party but soon caught up and commanded that the pots be overturned. Mohammed then divided the spoils of war with ten sheep equaling one camel.

"One camel escaped and the men chasing it soon became exhausted as there were few horses among us at the time. Finally a man shot an arrow, which Allah allowed to find its mark. Mohammed said, 'Some of these animals are like wild beasts, so if you can not control it, kill it.'

"Before dividing the animals among the soldiers, I said, 'We may seize animals in the future but lack knives. May we slaughter them with reeds?' Mohammed said, 'Use anything that causes blood to flow, and you may eat the meat if Allah's name be mentioned during slaughter. Do not use teeth or fingernails to slaughter animals. Teeth are really nothing but bones (do not cut correctly) and the Ethiopians use fingernails to slaughter meat, and we should not emulate Kafirs.'"

The Muslims had attacked the Hawazin tribe and taken their property and their wives and children as slaves. Then the Hawazin converted to Islam and came to Mohammed to try to get their families and property back. Since there will always be another jihad (until all the world submits to Islam) the jihadists could return the slaves and get their income from the next jihad.

B3,47,757 After a delegation from the Hawazin met with Mohammed, the prophet addressed the people, gave deserved thanks and praise to Allah, and said, "Your brothers have come begging forgiveness and freedom for their captured tribe members. I think it is reasonable that we grant it. If any of you will meet my request, I'll consider it a favor. If you choose to keep your share of the spoils of war until the next victory, then you will be reimbursed at that time." The audience responded, "As a favor to you, we will free those slaves."

Mohammed gave the Helpers (the Medinans who invited the Muslims to Medina and supported them in the days before jihad) no spoils of war in the taking of Mecca. Mohammed gave the new converts the Helpers' share to strengthen the faith of the new converts. Mohammed frequently used money to bond people to him.

B5,58,122 The day Mecca fell to the Muslims, Mohammed did not give a share of the spoils of war to the Helpers, instead distributing the wealth among new converts from the defeated Quraysh, the tribe of Mecca. The Helpers were overheard to say, "This isn't right. Our weapons are still red with the blood of the Quraysh, and they get our share of the spoils." When Mohammed learned of the dissatisfaction of the Helpers, he asked, "What is this grumbling that I'm hearing?" The Helpers admitted that they were indeed upset at the perceived slight. Mohammed said, "Doesn't it make you happy that while the Quraysh might bring spoils of war home with them, you get to take me into your homes?"

Mohammed used the spoils of war as a reward for those who were new to Islam. Money is one of the ways to influence those who are weak in Islam.

B4,53,373 Mohammed gave gifts to some and to others he did not. Those who did not receive gifts felt slighted and complained. Mohammed said, "I give presents to some people so that they do not stray from the path, or become disenchanted. Others simply need to be reminded of the wonder and pleasure Allah gives them. Amr is such a person." Amr said, "The words of the prophet are more valuable to me than red camels."

War treasure was a routine source of income to the jihadists.

B3,35,456 Abu Burda and Abdullah delegated me [Bin Abi] to inquire about rules governing the immediate payment for goods. They said, "When we accompanied Mohammed, we received spoils of war. We would pay the peasants of Sham in advance for goods and materials that would be delivered by a certain time." I asked, "Did the peasants own and maintain crop land for cultivation?" They answered, "We never asked."

Mohammed often used money to influence others about Islam.

B4,53,374 Mohammed: "I give money to the Quraysh to tempt them into remaining true to Islam, because they are new to the faith and their lives of ignorance are a short distance away."

As jihad grew and the wealth grew, Mohammed worried that the amount of wealth would corrupt the Muslims.

B5,59,351 Amr, who fought at the battle of Badr alongside Mohammed, said, "After Mohammed had concluded a peace treaty with Bahrain and named Al-Ala' their ruler, he deputized Abu Ubaida to go there and return with their submission tax payment [jizha]. When Abu Ubaida returned with the tribute, the Helpers, anticipating a dispersal of funds, met with Mohammed after morning prayers. Mohammed smiled upon seeing the Helpers and said, 'I believe you already know about Abu Ubaida's return.' They said, 'Yes.' Mohammed then said, 'Rejoice and wish for the things that make you happy. By Allah, I'm not afraid that you people will experience poverty, but I am afraid that you will handle success and riches just like others before you did. The competition for more wealth will turn you against each other and will destroy you as it did others before you.'"

To die in jihad is the best life.

B5,59,377 During the battle of Uhud, a man asked Mohammed, "Where will I go if I am killed in battle?" Mohammed said, "Paradise." The man then threw away the meal that he was carrying, joined the battle, and fought until he was killed.

Jihad is an obligation, not a recommendation. Allah demands jihad, now and forever, from all Muslims in all places and for all times.

B5,59,379 When the Koran was being compiled, I [Zaid] overlooked a verse that I had heard Mohammed recite. It was found after some searching. The verse read:

> 33:23 *Some among the believers have been faithful in their covenant with Allah. Some of them have fulfilled their covenant with their deaths, and some are waiting for death, and they have not wavered in their determination.*

We then added the verse to the Koran.

Jihad had to be waged far from Arabia and that meant fast transportation, so Mohammed used the rewards of jihad to build up his cavalry. He was a military genius who planned far ahead.

B5,59,537 The day Khaybar fell, Mohammed distributed the spoils by giving one share to the fighter and two shares to the owner of a horse. Nafi', a sub-narrator, elaborated, saying, "If a warrior supplied his own horse he received three shares; if he did not have a horse, he received only one."

Although Muslims can get to Paradise without jihad, jihadists will dwell in the highest levels there. Those who do not enter jihad must be judged on the Final Day. Their outcome is uncertain and they will suffer punishment of the grave. The jihadist goes straight to Paradise without judgment or suffering.

B4,52,48 Mohammed said, "Allah will accept anyone into Paradise who accepts Allah as the one god and Mohammed as His prophet, prays strictly according to ritual, and fasts during Ramadan, even if he didn't fight jihad or make a pilgrimage." The people asked, "Shall we tell the people the good news?" Mohammed said, "There are one hundred levels in Paradise reserved for jihadis who fight for Allah. The difference between one level and the next is comparable to the distance between Heaven and Earth. Therefore, when you request something from Allah, request the highest level of Paradise."

The very best of rewards awaits the martyrs of jihad.

B4,52,49 Mohammed said, "I dreamt last night that two men forced me to climb a tree whereupon I was taken into a wonderful house, the like of which I have never seen. One man said, 'This is the house of martyrs.'"

One fight in Allah's Cause is better than the rewards of the entire world.

B4,52,53 Mohammed: "Nobody who died and went to Paradise would want to return to life even if he were given the world and all its possessions, the exception being the martyr who recognized the moral superiority of giving his life for Allah and who wished to return to life only to give it again. A single act of jihad in the afternoon or morning is greater than the entire world and everything in it. A place in Paradise, no matter how small, is greater than the entire world and everything in it. If a houri [a virgin of Paradise devoted to perfect sexual satisfaction] came from Paradise and revealed herself to man, she would fill the sky between heaven and earth with bright light and sweet aromas. The veil she wears is greater than the entire earth and everything in it."

No matter how little a Muslim does, if he dies in jihad, he will be given the highest rewards. Good works and morality pale in comparison to the rewards of jihad.

B4,52,63 A man, his face shielded by his helmet, asked Mohammed, "Should I join the battle or accept Islam first?" Mohammed answered, "Accept Allah and then join the fight." The man accepted Islam and was killed shortly after. Mohammed said, "A small effort but a great prize. Even though he did not do much after accepting Islam, he shall be richly rewarded."

Mohammed was the perfect jihadist, and those who remember him (imitate him) will be given victory by Allah.

B4,52,146 Mohammed: "There will come a time when men leaving for jihad will be asked, 'Did any of you fight alongside Mohammed?' They will answer, 'Yes.' Allah will then grant them victory over the Kafir. Later there will come a time when men leaving for jihad will be asked, 'Did any of you fight alongside the men who fought alongside Mohammed?' They will answer, 'Yes,' and Allah will grant them victory. Then there will come a time when people will ask, 'Did any of you fight alongside the men who fought alongside the men who fought alongside Mohammed?' They will answer, 'Yes,' and victory will be granted them also."

Slaves were a part of jihad.

B4,53,344 When Fatima, Mohammed's daughter, received word that Mohammed had been given a number of slave girls as his share of spoils of war, she hoped that her strains from manual labor might be relieved. When she could not find Mohammed, Fatima told Aisha, Mohammed's favorite wife, that she wished to have a maid. Aisha passed her request to Mohammed, who visited the women after they had gone to bed. When they arose to greet him, Mohammed said, "Stay where you are." Mohammed put his foot on Fatima's chest and said, "Do you want to know what is better than a maid? Before going to bed, say, 'Allah is Great,' thirty-four times. Say, 'All praise to Allah,' thirty-three times, and say, 'Glory to Allah,' thirty-three times. This is better than asking for a maid."

Enslavement of the Kafirs and theft of their property were made sacred for Mohammed. Since Mohammed is the ideal pattern of behavior for all Muslims at all times and all places, the wealth of Kafirs is meant to be taken by others in Islam.

B4,53,351 Mohammed: "Allah has made it legal for me to take spoils of war."

Allah has a contractual agreement with all jihadists. If they die in jihad, Allah will reward them above all people. If they don't die, then they can profit by theft. So the jihadist has guarantees of profit in both this world and the next.

B4,53,352 Mohammed: "Allah promises the jihadi with pure intent either a place in Paradise or a return to his home with spoils of war and the guarantee of Allah's reward in the afterlife."

The wealth of Islam comes from what is taken from the Kafirs after jihad.

B4,53,358 During the battle of Al-Jamal, Az-Zubair looked over the battle field, called me [Abdulla, his son] to him and said as we stood there, "My son, people are going to be killed today. Some will be oppressors, some will be oppressed. I will be killed as an oppressed one. My greatest concern is my debts. Do you believe that we will have any money left after paying off all my notes?" He then added, "Son, sell our assets and settle my debts."

Although Az-Zubair never held a lucrative post, he saved his shares of spoils of war that had been allotted to him during battles alongside Mohammed, Abu Bakr, Umar, and Uthman....Anxious to gain their father's wealth, Az-Zubair's sons said, "Give us our inheritance now." Az-Zubair said, "No, by Allah. You won't get your inheritance until I have announced at four consecutive pilgrimages a call for anyone with money claims against me to come and allow me to settle the debt." After four years of doing so, Az-Zubair distributed his estate among his sons and his four wives. The value of the estate was 50,200,000 dinars [a fortune from the spoils of war of jihad].

The warrior gets the reward of the property of those he kills, so jihad can make the fighter wealthy. Many of Mohammed's followers became professional jihadists, which meant all of their income was from war on the Kafirs.

B4,53,370 During the battle of Hunain, I [Abu Qatada] was in the company of Mohammed. After the battle was joined, the Muslim army had begun to retreat when I saw a Kafir attacking a Muslim. I attacked him from behind and dealt him a mortal blow, though he almost killed me before he expired.

Following Umar, I asked him, "Why are the people fleeing?" "It is the will of Allah," he said. When the soldiers returned, Mohammed said, "Anyone who can prove that he killed an enemy soldier may have the dead man's possessions."

I rose and asked, "Who will be my witness?" before sitting down again. Mohammed repeated, "Anyone who can prove that he killed an enemy soldier may have the dead man's possessions." I stood up again and asked, "Who will be my witness?" Mohammed announced for a third time his call for claims and for the third time asked for a witness. Mohammed asked me, "Abu Qatada, what do you have to say?" After telling him the whole story, a man got up and said, Mohammed, "He is telling the truth. I have the dead man's possessions. Please compensate the man for me."

Abu Bakr spoke up, "No, by Allah, Mohammed will not give you the spoils of war won by a warrior who fights on behalf of Allah and

Mohammed." Mohammed said, "Abu Bakr is correct." So Mohammed gave me the man's armor, which I sold. I bought a garden with the money I received for the armor. It was the first property I acquired after my conversion to Islam.

SEX

Forced sex with the female captives of jihad was standard practice for Mohammed and his companions. These captives became slaves used for sex, and Mohammed had his choice of the most attractive new slaves. This is the ideal pattern of Islam.

B3,34,431 One of the captives was a beautiful Jewess, Safiya. Dihya had her first, but she was given to Mohammed next.

Mohammed accepted the forced sex with Kafirs.

B3,34,432 While sitting with Mohammed, I [Abu Said Al-Khudri] asked, "Mohammed, sometimes we receive female slaves as our share of the spoils. Naturally, we are concerned about their retaining their value [the sex slaves were worth less money if they were pregnant when sold]. How do you feel about *coitus interruptus*?" Mohammed asked, "Do you do that? It is better not to do that. It is Allah's will whether or not a child is born."

B7,62,9 I [Ibn Masud] and some of the soldiers who fought alongside Mohammed did not have wives, so we asked Mohammed, "Should we get castrated?" He forbade us.

Mohammed did not discourage forced sex but said if Allah wanted the slaves to be pregnant then nothing could prevent it. There are many prohibitions about sex in Islam, but none of them applies to sex with slaves.

B9,93,506 The Muslims captured some females during the battle of Bani Al-Mustaliq and planned to rape them but did not want them impregnated. They asked Mohammed if there were any restrictions against *coitus interruptus*. Mohammed told them that it was better that they should not interrupt their ejaculation. "It is preferable that you not do it because Allah has already determined everyone who will be born until the end of time." Mohammed said, "No life will be created if Allah does not create it."

M008,3371 Abu Sirma asked, "Abu Sa'id, did you ever hear Mohammed speak of *coitus interruptus*?" He answered, "Yes," and elaborated. "On expedition with Mohammed to the Bi'l-Mustaliq we captured several fine Arab women. As our wives were not with us, we very strongly wanted to rape the women but were concerned that a pregnant captive would be devalued. So we asked Mohammed whether we should practice *azl* [*coitus interruptus*] when raping the captives. Mohammed said that it did not matter because, if a soul is meant to be born, it will be born."

M008,3432 After the battle of Hunain, Mohammed attacked Autas. The companions of Mohammed achieved victory and took many captives, including many women, and they were reluctant to have sex with the captive women because their husbands were polytheists and held as captives nearby. Allah then revealed to Mohammed,

> 4:24 *You are also forbidden to marry two sisters at the same time, with the exception of those whom you have already married [married before the Koran]. Truly Allah is forgiving and merciful!* Also forbidden *to you are married women unless they are your slaves. This is the command of Allah. Other than those mentioned, all other women are lawful to you to court with your wealth and with honorable intentions, not with lust. And give those you have slept with a dowry, as it is your duty. But after you have fulfilled your duty, it is not an offense to make additional agreements among you. Truly Allah is knowing and wise!* [emphasis added]

BATTLES

In his last nine years Mohammed was involved in sixty-five events of violence, an average of one violent event every seven weeks. This total does not include acts of summary execution and assassinations.

The Jews of Khaybar were warned that they had been called to submit to Islam. They refused, and they were destroyed and made dhimmis (semi-slaves).

B5,59,285 Once, Zaid and I [Abu Ishaq] were sitting together, and someone asked him, "How many battles did Mohammed wage for Allah?" Zaid replied, "Nineteen." He was then asked, "How many battles did you fight alongside the Prophet?" He answered, "Seventeen." I asked him, "What was the first battle you fought alongside Mohammed?" Zaid said, "Al-Ashira or Al-Ashiru."

B1,11,584 When Mohammed led us into battle, he did not let us attack at night; instead he had us wait until morning. If morning prayers were heard he would delay the assault, and if the prayers were not heard, then the attack would commence.

After reaching Khaybar during the night we waited until morning to hear if they called to prayer. When the call was not heard, we rode into battle with Abi Talha ahead and Mohammed and me side by side.

The people of Khaybar were emerging from the town carrying their tools when they saw us. They screamed, "Mohammed! Oh my god, Mohammed's army!" Mohammed saw them and said, "Allah is great! Allah is great! Khaybar is destroyed." When we rode against a Kafir country, those people whom we had warned were in for an evil morning.

B3,41,589 Once while campaigning with Mohammed I [Jabir] was riding a camel that became fatigued and began to fall behind. Mohammed struck the beast and said, "Sell me this camel. You may continue to ride it until we reach Medina."

As we drew close to Medina, I asked permission from Mohammed to ride ahead to my house to visit my new bride. Mohammed asked, "Did you marry a virgin or a woman who had been married before?" I answered, "I married a matron. My father, Abdullah, is dead, so I wanted someone who could properly raise and instruct my young sisters." Mohammed said, "Go see your family."

When I reached my home, my uncle scolded me for selling the camel, despite my account of its slow pace and weak condition and the beating it took from Mohammed. When Mohammed reached Medina a short time later, I took the camel to him. He gave me the agreed upon price and my share of the war spoils and told me to keep the camel also.

Jihad is a sacred act, and it should not interfere with prayer. But war demands practicality, so the jihadist should practice Islam so that it does not endanger the goals of jihad.

B2,14,65 Ibn Umar:

When Muslims and Kafirs face each other in battle, Muslims may pray without prostrating themselves. Ibn Umar added, "Mohammed said, 'If the enemy outnumbers our forces, the Muslim soldier may pray while standing or riding a mount.'"

Safiya was the most beautiful of the Jews. Mohammed assassinated her husband, killed her cousins, and tortured her father to death.

B2,14,68 During the night Mohammed said the Fajr prayer, mounted his beast and said, "God is great! Khaybar is destroyed! When we ride against a nation that has ignored our warning, they are in for the most terrible morning." As the people emerged from the city and saw our forces, they screamed the warning, "Mohammed and his army are here." Mohammed crushed them, killing their warriors and seizing their women and children. Dihya Al-Kalbi took Safiya, although she was later given to Mohammed, who married her and gave her her freedom as a wedding present.

Jihadists do not fear death and are brave.

B2,23,338 Mohammed said, "Zaid was our flag bearer and was killed. Jafar took the flag and was also killed. Abdullah then took the flag, but he was killed also," and Mohammed's eyes filled with tears. "Khalid then took the flag, though he was not yet a chief, and Allah blessed him with victory."

Though Mohammed would mourn the death of Muslims, there is not a recorded event where he expressed any regret or remorse at the death and suffering of any Kafir opponent.

B2,23,387 I never saw Mohammed sadder than he was the day that the reciters of the Koran [men who had memorized the Koran] were killed. He prayed for an entire month for the destruction of his enemies.

B2,23,452 After the battle of Badr, the bodies of the Kafirs were thrown in a well where Mohammed addressed them, "Do you still believe the promises of your god?" Somebody said, "You are talking to dead people." Mohammed answered, "They hear as well as you, but they can't talk back."

Mecca had been a town of sanctuary before Islam, and Ibn Khatal was there seeking refuge as an apostate.

B3,29,72 When Mohammed entered Mecca after its fall to the Muslims, he removed the Arabian helmet he was wearing, signaling the end of the battle. Someone came to him and said, "Ibn Khatal has sought refuge in the Kabah." Mohammed said, "Kill him."

The enemies of Islam will be destroyed.

B3,38,498 Abdur-Rahman brokered an agreement between Umaiya and me, whereby I would protect his family and property in Medina if he would protect my property and family in Mecca. In the contract, I referred to myself by my Islamic name, Ar-Rahman', which Umaiya did not recognize. He said, "Write down your pre-Islamic name." I signed the document, Abdu Amr'.

After the battle of Badr, during the night, I climbed the hill to protect Umaiya. Bilal saw him and called to a group of Helpers saying, "There is Umaiya! I am in trouble if he escapes." Bilal and the Helpers began to chase us, and Umaiya and Abdur-Rahman began to fear that they would catch us. I ordered Umaiya's son to slow their advance, but he was quickly killed and the group pressed on. Umaiya was very fat, and it became obvious that we could not escape. I told him to kneel and I covered his body with my own to protect him, but the Helpers drove their weapons underneath me killing him and slicing my foot.

The Jews were date farmers. One of the tactics of jihad is to attack economic assets [this was a goal of September 11, 2001 attack].

B3,39,519 Mohammed destroyed the date orchards of the Jews and Hassan wrote this poetic verse: "The chiefs of Bani LuAi enjoyed watching the Jew's trees consumed by fire."

B3,48,832 The night before the battle of Uhud, Mohammed ordered me to present myself before him. I was fourteen at the time, and he did not allow me to fight in that battle. I was fifteen when he called me before him on the eve of the battle of the Trench, and he gave his permission for me to fight. Nafi' said, "I told this story to Umar, who was caliph at the time, and he said, 'Fifteen is the boundary between boyhood and manhood.' He then wrote his governors telling them to pay salaries to jihadists when they reach fifteen.

All of the earth is the domain of Islam, and all of the wealth of the world belongs to Islam. The only safety from jihad is to become a Muslim.

B4,53,392 Leaving the Mosque one day Mohammed said, "Let's go speak to the Jews." When we arrived Mohammed said, "You will be safe if you accept Islam. The earth belongs to Allah and myself, and I want you out of here. If you own any property, you may sell it, but you need to know that the world belongs to Allah and Mohammed."

It is a duty to kill those who resist Islam. Killing in jihad is a blessing.

B5,58,160 Before Islam became supreme, there was a house called Dhul-Khalasa. Mohammed asked me, "Will you take care of Dhul-Khalasa for me?" I took one hundred and fifty riders with me and destroyed the house and killed everyone we found. When we returned and reported back to Mohammed, he called upon Allah to bless us.

B5,59,287 Kab fought alongside Mohammed in every battle except Tabuk. I, myself did not participate in the battle of Badr, but no blame was attached to myself or others who missed that battle because Mohammed had left to meet the Quraysh caravans, and the battle was quite unplanned and unexpected.

B5,59,288 Ibn Masud saw Al-Miqdad do something that I wish more than anything I had done. Mohammed was rousing the Muslims to join battle with the Kafirs, when Al-Miqdad joined him and said, "We will not be like the Jews, who said:

5:24 *They said, "O, Moses, we will never enter while they remain there. You and your Lord should go and fight. We will sit here and watch.*

Instead, we will stand with you on your right and your left, in the vanguard and at your back." That saying delighted him, and I saw his face get bright with happiness.

It is the will of Allah that Islam should triumph in jihad.

B5,59,289 Before the battle of Badr, Mohammed prayed, "Allah, I beseech you to honor your promise and agreement with us. If you desire that no one worship you, then let the Kafirs triumph." Abu Bakr then took him by his hand and said, "You have done enough." Mohammed then said,

54:45 *They will be routed and will turn their backs and run.*

A war story:

B5,59,311 Az-Zubair had three scars from battle, one of which was so deep that I [Urwa] used to put my fingers in it. Two of those wounds he received at the battle of Badr and the other at the battle of Al-Yarmuk. When Abdullah was killed, Abdul-Malik asked me, "Urwa, do you recognize Az-Zubair's sword?" I responded, "Of course." He asked, "What distinguishing marks does it have?" I said, "It was dented on the blade edge at the battle of Badr." Abdul-Malik said, "That's right! The sword is dented from fighting the Kafirs." Abdul-Malik then returned the sword to me.

Hisham, Urwa's son said, "The sword's value was estimated at three thousand dinars before it was given to one of Az-Zubair's heirs. I wish that it were mine."

Allah will punish those who die defending themselves and their culture against Islam.

B5,59,314 After the battle of Badr, Mohammed ordered that the bodies of twenty-four slain Quraysh leaders be dumped in an abandoned well. As was his custom following the conquest of a city, Mohammed remained on the battlefield for three nights. After the third night following the battle, Mohammed rode out, followed by his companions, who said to themselves, "He is riding with some purpose in mind."

When Mohammed reached the dry well, he began to speak to the corpses of his enemies, addressing them by their names and the names of their fathers. "O so and so, son of so and so! Would you be happy today if you had submitted to Allah and me? Our god has kept his promises. Has your god kept his promises to you?"

Umar said, "Mohammed, you are talking to soulless corpses." Mohammed said, "By Allah, you do not hear my words any better than they." (Qatada said, "Allah resurrected them so that they might hear Mohammed's scoldings and insults and feel remorse and regret.")

Violence determines truth in Islam.

B5,59,316 Aisha says this quote was attributed by Ibn Umar to Mohammed: "The dead are punished because of the grieving of their families." Aisha, however, said, "But Mohammed said, 'The dead are punished for their transgressions while their families grieve.'" She also said, "This is much like the words spoken by Mohammed to the corpses in the well at Badr, 'They hear my words.'" And she said, "He said, 'Now they know that I was telling the truth.'"

B5,59,322 At the battle of Badr, Muslim forces captured seventy Kafirs and killed another seventy. At the battle of Mount Uhud, when Mohammed named Abdullah chief of archers and seventy Muslims were either killed or wounded, Abu Sufyan said, "This day is their revenge for our victory at Badr. The outcome of the war is still to be determined."

The war trophies of jihad:

B5,59,333 Az-Zubair said, "At the battle of Badr, I came face to face with Ubaida, who was covered with armor, only his eyes being unprotected. Ubaida, surnamed Abu Dhat-Al-Karish, proudly said, 'I am Abu-Al-Karish.' I struck him in the eye with my spear, killing him. The spear was bent and consequently very difficult to dislodge. I put my foot on his corpse and yanked it free." Urwa said, "Mohammed later asked Az-Zubair for that spear, and he gave it to him. When Mohammed died, the spear was given back to Az-Zubair. Abu Bakr then demanded the spear, and Az-Zubair gave it to him. After Abu Bakr died the spear was returned to Az-Zubair. Umar then asked for the sword, and it was given to him. When Umar died, the spear was again returned to Az-Zubair before Uthman demanded it. After Uthman was killed, the spear stayed with Ali's heirs. The son of Az-Zubair then demanded it back, and it remained in his possession until he was killed in battle.

No amount of suffering will discourage the jihadists.

B8,76,460 Sa'd was the first Arab to wage jihad. He said, "At times during jihad, there was nothing to eat except the leaves of desert trees. Our waste resembled that of a sheep. Nowadays, the Bani Asad instruct me in the rules of Islam. If I have to listen to them, I am done for, and all of my suffering has been wasted."

This next hadith is of great importance. Amir killed himself while trying to kill Kafirs during jihad. Suicide is a crime against Allah and a sentence to Hell. His fellow jihadists said that since he had killed himself he was lost. Mohammed said that killing oneself in jihad is not suicide and instead earns the jihadist the highest reward.

Kafirs today call such jihadists "suicide bombers" but that is not accurate. The formal name for those who try to commit suicide in the name of jihad is *mujahadeen* and for those who succeed it is *shaeen*.

Some Muslims claim that since suicide is against Islam the human bombers are not Islamic. That statement is an example of *taqiyya* (sacred deceit).

Suicide is a sin in Islam, but killing oneself in jihad is not considered suicide; it is actually the highest form of Islam.

B9,83,29 Our company was traveling to Khaybar with Mohammed when someone called out, "Amir, sing some of your camel-driving songs." He complied, singing several songs whose rhythm mimicked the gait of camels. Mohammed was pleased and asked, "Who is that man?" "Amir," someone told him. Mohammed then said, "May Allah show mercy to him." Several of us said, "Mohammed, we hope that you will let him stay with us for a while," but he was killed early the next day.

We were very upset. Several people remarked, "It is too bad that all of Amir's good deeds have gone to waste, because he is damned for killing himself." When I heard those remarks, I went to Mohammed and said, "Prophet of Allah, I would sacrifice my father for you, but the people say that Amir is damned." Mohammed said, "Then those people lie. Amir will be doubly rewarded because he strove to be obedient to Allah, and he fought in jihad. No other death would bring so great a reward."

Being killed in jihad makes Allah happy.

B4,52,57 Mohammed sent seventy men to preach Islam to the Bani Amir. Upon arriving, my mother's brother said to them, "I will go first, and if they let me preach the word of Allah, everything will be alright, if not, then stay close to me. He went ahead and they promised him protection. However, while he was preaching the word of Allah, the Bani Amir ordered one of their men to kill him. My uncle cried, "Allah is supreme! By the Lord of the Kabah, I have completed my task."

The Bani Amir then attacked and killed all but a lame man who escaped to the mountain. Gabriel told Mohammed that the martyrs had met Allah, and that He was pleased with them and that pleased the martyrs." We used to recite a Koranic verse that was later cancelled: "Tell the people that we have met Allah and He is happy with us and He has made us happy." Mohammed called upon Allah for forty days to curse the Bani Amir for disobeying Allah and Mohammed.

Mohammed as a battlefield general:

B4,52,149 Abu Usaid, "At the battle of Badr, when the Muslim army was arrayed against the army of Quraysh, Mohammed said, "When they come near, let fly your arrows at them.""

In the hour of final judgment by Allah, those killed by jihad will find that death was small compared to eternal punishment for resisting Islam. First, the jihadist causes suffering and death; then Allah causes suffering for eternity.

B4,52,164 Mohammed sat in his tent shortly before the battle of Badr and said, "Allah, I beg you to honor our contract and your promise. If you wish our destruction, you will never be worshiped again." Abu Bakr grabbed his hand and said, "That will do, Mohammed! You have vigorously pleaded with Allah." Mohammed, clad in armor, went out and said to me:

> 54:45 *They will be routed and will turn their backs and run. No! The Hour of Judgment is their promised time, and that hour will be terrible and bitter.*

Khalid confirms that this occurred at the battle of Badr.

Mohammed used deception with his enemies.

B4,52,198 When Mohammed planned an attack, he would use deceit to conceal his objective. (Ka'b would say, "Mohammed rarely began an attack on any day but Thursday.") The exception being the battle of Tabuk which was fought during extremely hot weather. Facing a long trek through the desert before attacking a formidable host, Mohammed told his army their destination and made clear their difficult situation.

Allegiance to Islam is allegiance to death.

B4,52,207 I [Salama] promised loyalty to Mohammed and then cooled myself in the shadow of a tree. As the crowd around Mohammed began to thin, he asked, "Ibn Al-Akwa! Will we do so again?" So I pledged my allegiance to him a second time. I asked, "Abu Muslim, what kind of pledge did you give Mohammed?" He answered, "I pledged my death."

B4,52,208 At the battle of the Trench, the Helpers were heard to say, "We promise Mohammed to wage jihad until death." Mohammed said, "Allah, there is no life except the life after death. Honor the Helpers and the Emigrants with your bounty."

Mujashi narrated: My brother and I went to Mohammed and asked to take the pledge to migrate. He replied, "There is no need for that any more." I asked, "What may we pledge to you?" He answered, "Take the pledge to accept Islam and wage jihad."

In jihad, patience is a virtue.

B4,52,210 Once during battle, Mohammed spoke to the people as the sun was going down and said, "Do not willingly go into battle and beg Allah to protect you from harm. If you do go into battle, have patience and remember that Paradise lies in the shadow of swords." Mohammed then said, "Allah, bestower of the Koran, master of the elements, conqueror of the pagans, defeat the Kafir and give us victory."

The call to submit to Islam always precedes the attack. [Osama Bin Laden called America to Islam in his recorded speech before the September 11, 2001 attack.]

B4,52,253 On the eve of the Battle of Khaybar, Mohammed said, "Tomorrow I will give the flag to a man to whom Allah will grant victory." Everybody wondered who would be chosen flag bearer, and of course each hoped it would be him. In the morning, Mohammed asked, "Where is Ali?" Told that Ali had an ailment of the eyes, Mohammed went and treated him with saliva and prayed to Allah for a cure. Immediately Ali recovered. Taking the flag from Mohammed, Ali asked, "Do I fight them until they submit to Islam?" Mohammed said, "Ride with patience and calm until you enter their land, then ask them to submit to Allah and teach them what is forbidden. If Allah grants insight to someone through you, your reward is greater than if you were given red camels."

A tactical mission.

B4,52,259 While giving orders for a mission he wished us to undertake, Mohammed said, "If you find so-and-so, burn them with fire." Just as we were leaving, however, Mohammed said, "Although I have ordered you to burn those two men, I realize only Allah may punish with fire, so if you do find them, just kill them."

Assassination is a tactic of jihad and was used frequently by Mohammed. Not one person in Arabia who opposed or criticized Mohammed lived except by fleeing or converting. Assassinations were common and feared.

B4,52,265 Mohammed ordered a band of Helpers to assassinate Abu Rafi. One of the group, Abdullah, slipped into his house at night and killed him in his sleep."

All Kafirs who resist in any way can be killed as an act of jihad.

B4,52,286 Mohammed was traveling one time when a Kafir spy came to him. After sitting and talking a while with Mohammed and his companions, the spy departed. Mohammed said, "Chase him down and kill him." So, I [Al Akwa] did. Mohammed rewarded me with the spy's possessions and his share of the spoils.

Those who support jihad by caring for families of jihadists are equal to them.

B4,53,359 Uthman did not participate in the battle of Badr because his wife, a daughter of Mohammed, was ill. Mohammed said to him, "You will be rewarded and given a share of the spoils just as if you had participated in the battle."

The spoils of war.

B4,53,362 Abdullah Bin Umar was in a detachment sent by Mohammed to Najd. They captured a large number of camels. Each of them was given eleven or twelve as his share and given an extra camel as a bonus.

Captives could be killed or ransomed.

B4,53,367 Speaking about the captives from the battle of Badr, Mohammed said, "If Al-Mutim were alive and if he asked me to, I would have freed those people for his sake."

Abu Jahl spoke against Mohammed, so he was marked for killing. Only those who submit are safe.

B4,53,369 At the battle of Badr, I, Abdur-Rahman, stood in the front line between two young boys and wished that I had been the stronger man. One of them got my attention and said, "Uncle, do you know Abu Jahl?" I said, "Yes, why do you ask?" He replied, "People tell me he speaks ill of Mohammed. By Allah, if I see him, I will not break off my attack until one of us is dead."

I was shocked to hear this. Then the other boy said the same thing to me. Sometime later, I saw Abu Jahl, and I pointed him out to the boys, saying, "There is the man you seek." After ferociously attacking and killing him, the boys went to Mohammed and told him of Abu Jahl's death. Mohammed asked, "Who killed him?" They both truthfully said, "I have killed him." Mohammed asked, "Did you clean your swords?" After they answered, "No," Mohammed glanced at their swords and said, "Obviously, you both killed him, so his possessions will be divided between the two of you."

Treaties are a part of jihad. The treaty of Hudaibiya recognized Islam as a political power, but the protection it offered to the Kafirs was voided after

Mohammed became strong enough to crush his opponents. Treaties are an element of strategy for giving Islam time to gain strength. In the end only submission will stop jihad.

B4,53,406 While in Siffin, Sahl arose and scolded the people saying, "Brothers, accept blame. We stood alongside of Mohammed at Hudaibiya, we would have fought if we had been asked to." Then Umar came to Mohammed and questioned him, "Mohammed, are we not right and our enemies wrong?" "Yes," Mohammed said. Umar asked, "Do not our slain soldiers reside in Paradise while theirs burn in Hell?" Mohammed said, "Yes." Exasperated, Umar asked, "Then why should we accept a bad treaty that limits Islam? Will this treaty last until Allah judges between the believers and the non-believers?" Mohammed said, "Ibn Al-Khattab, I am the prophet of Allah. Allah will never diminish me."

Umar then went to Abu Bakr and repeated the concerns he expressed to Mohammed. Abu Bakr said to him, "Mohammed is the prophet of Allah and Allah will never diminish him." The Victory sura of the Koran was then revealed to Mohammed who recited it in its entirety to Umar. Umar then asked, "Mohammed, was the treaty of Hudaibiya really a victory for Islam?" Mohammed said, "Yes."

No death is too painful or fearful for the Kafir. Allah will be even more cruel in Hell for eternity.

B8,82,795 Mohammed punished the men of the Uraina tribe by cutting off their hands and feet and letting them bleed to death.

Jihad is obligatory for a Muslim. Jihad was not just for the days of Mohammed but forever. The only proper response to jihad is immediate obedience to the call and need.

B4,53,41 On the day Mecca fell, Mohammed said, "There is no longer a need to migrate, but the necessity for jihad remains and so does the need for pure intent. When you are called to jihad, you should come immediately."

Mohammed also said that day, "When Allah created the heavens and the earth, he made Mecca a sanctuary. Before me, fighting was forbidden here, and Allah has made it legal for me only for this time.

"By Allah's order Mecca is a sanctuary until Judgment day. Its weeds should not be chopped, its animals should not be hunted, its lost belongings should not be disturbed except by someone who will publicly seek its true owner, and its grass should not be plowed."

Hearing that, Al-Abbas said, "Mohammed, What about the Idhkhir? It is used by the people to build their homes and by the goldsmiths." Mohammed then said, "Idhkhir is the exception."

Only Mohammed could kill in Mecca.

B1,3,104 Amr was gathering troops to send to Mecca to fight Abdullah when I [Abu Shuraih] said to him, "Chief, may I relate to you the words of Mohammed on the day Mecca fell to Islam's forces? I personally witnessed the speech, and there was no mistaking its meaning. He gave thanks and praise to Allah and said, 'Allah has made Mecca a sanctuary, not man. A Muslim must not even fell its trees, let alone shed blood on its sacred ground. If anyone says that it is permissible to fight there just as Mohammed did, then let them know that Allah granted permission to his prophet, but He did not give it to them.' Mohammed also said, 'Allah gave me permission to violate the sanctity of Mecca for only those few hours; now it is as inviolate as it was before that day. It is necessary that those of you who are here now share this information with those not present.'"

Abu was asked, "What did Amr say?" Amr said, "Abu, I know better than you. Mecca gives no protection to men who disobey Allah, or to thieves or murderers that run to her walls seeking refuge."

MISCELLANEOUS

Kafirs can advance Islam.

B8,77,603 We witnessed, along with Allah's Apostle, the Khaybar campaign. Allah's Apostle told his companions about a man who claimed to be a Muslim, "This man is from the people of the Fire [Zoroastrian]."

When the battle started, the man fought very bravely and received a great number of wounds and got crippled. On that, a man from among the companions of the Prophet came and said, "O Allah's Apostle! Do you know what the man you described as of the people of the Fire has done? He has fought very bravely for Allah's Cause and he has received many wounds, the Prophet said, "But he is indeed one of the people of the Fire."

Some of the Muslims were about to have some doubt about that statement. So while the man was in that state, the pain caused by the wounds troubled him so much that he put his hand into his quiver and took out an arrow and committed suicide with it. Off went some men from among the Muslims to Allah's Apostle and said, "O Allah's Apostle! Allah has made your statement true. So-and-so has committed suicide."

Allah's Apostle said, "O Bilal! Get up and announce in public: None will enter Paradise but a believer, and Allah may support Islam with a wicked man."

B3,30,114 Umar said, "Allah, Let me die fighting for you, and let my end come in Mecca."

M020,4711 Mohammed: "Be ready to meet them with as much strength as you can muster. Remember, power rests in archery. Remember, power rests in archery. Remember, power rests in archery."

B5,59,400 Pointing to his broken front tooth, Mohammed said, "Allah's rage is severe on those who harmed His apostle. Allah's rage is severe on the man slain by His apostle during jihad."

M021,4810 I [Shaddid B. Aus] remember two things Mohammed said, "Allah has commanded that every act be good; if you must kill, kill in a good way and when you butcher, butcher in a good way. All of you should keep your blades sharp, and allow the slaughtered beast (man or animal) to die as comfortably as possible."

Here we see that Mohammed used propaganda as one of Islam's most valuable weapons of jihad. Allah supports propaganda and the debasement of Kafirs.

B5,59,449 Mohammed said to Hassan, "Insult them [the Kafirs] with your poetry and Gabriel will protect you."

M031,6074 Mohammed said, "Hassan B. Thibit, satirize and mock the Kafir; Gabriel is by your side." This hadith was narrated with the authority of Shu'ba and the same line of transmitters.

Since Allah is the prime mover of jihad and actively helps jihadists, a very few jihadists can overcome superior forces. No enemy is too large or too strong for Islam. It is predestined that all opposition will be crushed by jihad. Only the time is unknown, not the final outcome.

B6,60,176 When the verse, "If there are twenty steadfast amongst you Muslims, they will overcome two hundred Kafirs," was revealed, it hurt the morale of the jihadists. A ten-to-one advantage was too much to fight against. When Allah reduced this demand by revealing to Mohammed:

> 8:66 *Allah has now lessened your burden because He knows that there is weakness in you. If there are among you a hundred men who will stand fast, they will overcome two hundred.*

Then their morale improved.

Islam must annihilate the ancient religions.

M031,6052 According to Jabir, before the Muslim conquest of Arabia, there was a temple named Dhu'l-Khalasash also called the northern Kabah, or the Yamanite Kabah. "Mohammed asked me, 'Will you take care of Dhu'l-Khalasah for me?' I agreed and led three hundred and fifty Ahmas cavalrymen on a mission to destroy the temple and kill everyone we could lay hands upon. We informed Mohammed of our success immediately upon our return, and he blessed us and the entire tribe of the Ahmazs."

Horses and jihad:

B9,92,454 Mohammed: "A horse may be used for three purposes: a man may use one to seek his reward in the afterlife, another man may use one to protect himself and his possessions, and still another man may use his horse for immoral purposes.

"The man whose horse brings him everlasting reward is the man who uses his horse for jihad. The most insignificant action by that horse, whether it be drinking water, or expelling waste, is a good deed and brings reward to the man who owns it.

"The man who uses his horse primarily to earn wages and preserve his independence, but also allows it to be used for jihad, owns a beast that guards him from need.

"The man who owns a horse merely to boast, or as a matter of pride, possesses a beast that only carries sin. When someone asked Mohammed about donkeys, he said, The only revelation from Allah about such a thing is contained in this verse:

> 99:7 *On that day men will come forward in droves to witness their deeds, and whoever has done even an atom's weight of good will see it, and whoever has done even an atom's weight of evil will see it.*"

B4,53,348 Mohammed: "Until Judgment day, horses will be a source of good: either Allah's reward in Paradise, or the spoils of war."

Jihad is the only sure path to Paradise.

B9,93,549 Mohammed said, "Allah promises that the Muslim who participates in jihad with no compulsion, other than true faith and the desire to serve Allah, will either be admitted into Paradise, or sent home with Allah's reward or a share of the spoils of war."

The remark of five words, "this is enough for me," was a death sentence for an old man.

B2,19,173 Mohammed would prostrate himself on the ground while reciting the Koran at Mecca. His companions followed his example [their piety was evident by the dirt on their foreheads] except for an old man who merely touched a handful of dirt and pebbles to his head and said, "This is enough for me." Soon after, I saw that man killed for being a Kafir.

The poetry of this hadith is the most elegant expression of jihad.

B4,52,73 Mohammed: "Be aware that Paradise lies under the shadow of swords."

Jihad should be waged at the right time. Haste should never be a priority.

B4,52,86 Mohammed: "When you prepare to fight your enemy, take your time."

To obey Mohammed is to obey Allah. To ignore the ideal life example of Mohammed is a sin against Islam and Allah. To obey the righteous imam is to obey Allah.

B4,52,204 Mohammed: "We may represent the last group of apostles of Allah, but we shall be the first to enter Paradise. If you obey me, then you obey Allah, and if you disobey me, then you disobey Allah. If you obey the chief, then you obey me, and if you disobey the chief, then you also disobey me. The imam is a fortress that Muslims should protect and where they should seek refuge. If the imam is just and righteous, then he will be rewarded by Allah, but if he is not, then he will held accountable."

Mohammed was the perfect jihadist.

B4,52,216 Mohammed: "If I did not have to worry about my disciples, I would never stay behind while soldiers march off to war. However, I don't have the means to transport them and I hate to leave them behind. Obviously, if I could I would fight and die in jihad, be resurrected and be martyred again."

War is deceit and jihad is deceit. Lies and deceit are one of the chief weapons of jihad.

B4,52,267 Mohammed: "The Persian king shall be killed, and there will not be another. Caesar will certainly be destroyed, and there will not be another, and you will exhaust their riches supporting jihad. War is deceit."

Here we see the value of long-range strategic thinking in jihad. This hadith teaches the reason of jihad. Islam came to Persia to become its master and destroy its culture.

B4,53,386 Umar ordered the Muslims to attack the Kafirs in the neighboring lands. When Al-Hurmuzan accepted Islam, Umar said, "Give me your advice about these countries I want to invade." Al-Hurmuzan said, "Certainly, these nations and people who reject Islam are like a bird. If we break one of its wings, then it could still get up using its head, other wing, and legs. If we were to break its other wing, then it could still get up using its head and legs. However, if we were to destroy its head, then the rest of the bird would be helpless. The head represents the Persian king, while one wing symbolizes Caesar and the other wing represents the Persian people. Therefore, order your troops to attack the Persian king."

Consequently, Umar appointed An-Numan as our commander and sent us to confront the ruler of Persia. When we arrived, we were met by forty thousand soldiers led by the Persian King's representative and an interpreter who said, "let one man speak." Al-Murghira answered, "Ask me anything." The Persian asked, "Who are you?" Al-Murghira said, "We are Arabs; we have led miserable lives. Hunger, thirst, poverty, and hardship were our daily fare. We worshiped rocks and trees until Allah sent to us a prophet from our own people.

Mohammed has ordered us to battle you until either you worship and accept Allah as the one God, or you recognize our dominance over you and pay tribute. Mohammed revealed to us that Allah said, "Any Muslim killed in battle shall be admitted into Paradise and a life of everlasting luxury and bliss. Whomever survives the battle shall make you their slave."

When Al-Mughira chided An-Numan for not immediately pressing the attack, An-Numan replied, "If you had fought alongside Mohammed in a similar battle he would not have faulted your delay, or belittled you. I, on the other hand, accompanied Mohammed at many such battles and it was customary for him to attack in the afternoon if he could not begin at day break."

The following hadith led to the Jewish-Arabian holocaust. The second rightly guided caliph, Umar, drove out every Jew and Christian from Arabia, based upon this hadith. The only Jews left behind were used for sexual slavery. To this day, church and synagogue are forbidden in Arabia—religious apartheid. The use of money to influence others for Islam was the other of two final commands.

B4,53,393 Bin Jubair overheard Ibn Abbas mourning, "Thursday! Oh, you remember what happened on Thursday." Ibn Abbas then wept till the earth was muddied with tears. I asked Ibn Abbas, "What is the significance of Thursday?" He said, "Mohammed was on his deathbed and he said, "Bring me something to write with so that I may leave you instructions to keep you on the right path after I die." Although it was improper to do so, those present argued amongst themselves in front of Mohammed. Some said, "What is his problem? Is he mad, or delirious?" Mohammed said, "Let me be. I am better off dying than listening to you."

Mohammed then gave three orders saying, "Drive all the Kafirs from Arabia and give gifts and respect to all foreign representatives just like I used to do." The secondary narrator concluded, "Either Ibn Abbas did not mention the third command, or I forgot what he said."

Here is a summary of jihad by Ibn Taymiya, a famous Islamic scholar of the fourteenth century:[1]

In ordering jihad Allah has said:

2:193 *Fight them until you are no longer persecuted and the religion of Allah reigns absolute*

Allah has, in fact, repeated this obligation [to fight] and has glorified jihad in most of the Medinan Suras; he has stigmatized those who neglected to fight in jihad and treated them as hypocrites and cowards.

It is impossible to count the number of times when jihad and its virtues are extolled in the Koran and the Sunna [Sira and Hadith]. Jihad is the best form of voluntary service that man consecrates to Allah.

Therefore, since jihad is divinely instituted with its goal of religion reverting in its entirety to Allah [all religions must submit to Islam], and to make Allah's word triumph, whoever opposes the realization of this goal will be fought, according to the unanimous opinion of Muslims.

Jews and Christians, as well as Zoroastrians (Magians, followers of the native religion of the Persians) must be fought until they embrace Islam or pay the jizya (submission tax of humiliation) without recriminations. Muslim legal experts do not agree on whether the jizya should be imposed on other categories of Kafirs or not; on the other hand, all consider that it should not be required of Arabs [hence they should convert to Islam or be killed or expelled].

This is the Sunna of Mohammed

---

1. Bat Ye'or, *Islam and Dhimmitude* (Associated University Press, Cranbury, NJ, 2003), 44.

THE TEARS OF JIHAD

These figures are a rough estimate of the death of Kafirs by the political act of jihad found in the Hadith.

AFRICANS

Thomas Sowell estimates that 11 million slaves were shipped across the Atlantic and 14 million were sent to the Islamic nations of North Africa and the Middle East[1]. For every slave captured many others died. Estimates of this collateral damage vary. The renowned missionary David Livingstone estimated that for every slave who reached the plantation five others died by being killed in the raid or died on the forced march from illness and privation[2]. So, for 25 million slaves delivered to the market, we have the death of about 120 million people. Islam ran the wholesale slave trade in Africa.[3]

120 million Africans

CHRISTIANS

The number of Christians martyred by Islam is 9 million[4]. A rough estimate by Raphael Moore in *History of Asia Minor* is that another 50 million died in wars by jihad. So to account for the 1 million African Christians killed in the 20th century we have:

60 million Christians

JEWS

The Jews had no political control over any country and their deaths were limited to a few thousand killed in riots.

---

1. Thomas Sowell, *Race and Culture*, BasicBooks, 1994, p. 188.
2. Woman's Presbyterian Board of Missions, *David Livingstone,* p. 62, 1888.
3 Bernard Lewis, *Race and Slavery in the Middle East*, Oxford University Press, 1990.
4. David B. Barrett, Todd M. Johnson, *World Christian Trends AD 30-AD 2200*, William Carey Library, 2001, p. 230, table 4-10.

HINDUS

Koenard Elst in *Negationism in India*[5] gives an estimate of 80 million Hindus killed in the total jihad against India. The country of India today is only half the size of ancient India, due to jihad. The mountains near India are called the Hindu Kush, meaning the "funeral pyre of the Hindus".

80 million Hindus

BUDDHISTS

Buddhists do not keep up with the history of war. Keep in mind that in jihad only Christians and Jews were allowed to survive as dhimmis (third-class citizens under Sharia); everyone else had to convert or die. Jihad killed the Buddhists in Turkey, Afghanistan, along the Silk Route, and in India. The total is roughly 10 million[6].

10 million Buddhists

TOTAL

This gives a rough estimate of 270 million killed by jihad.

---

5. Koenard Elst, *Negationism in India*, Voice of India, New Delhi, 2002, pg. 34.
6. David B. Barrett, Todd M. Johnson, *World Christian Trends AD 30-AD 2200*, William Carey Library, 2001, p. 230, table 4-1.

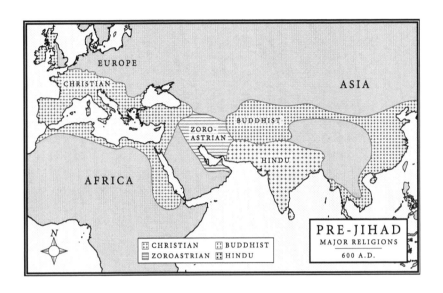

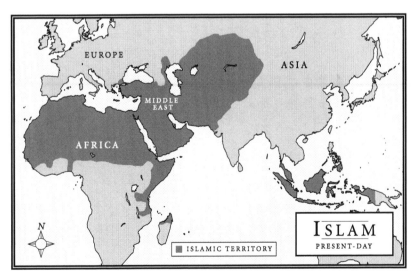

THE DHIMMIS

CHAPTER 4

5:92 Obey Allah, and obey the Messenger, and be on your
guard. If you do turn back, know that our Messenger
is only bound to deliver a plain announcement.

Mohammed took his army a hundred miles from Medina to Khaybar and attacked the Jews. Islam was totally victorious. After taking the property of the Jews as the spoils of war, the Muslims made an agreement called a *dhimma* with the Jews in Arabia. The Jews could stay and farm the land if they gave Islam half their profits. They then became *dhimmis* who were under the protection of Islam.

Thus the word dhimmi came to mean permanent, second-class Kafir citizens in a country ruled by Islam. Dhimmis paid a special tax, and their civil and legal rights were greatly limited. The only way out of being a dhimmi was to convert to Islam or flee. The taxes from the dhimmis made Islam rich.

There are very few hadiths about dhimmitude, but it was another of Mohammed's unique political inventions. The scorched-earth policy of killing all Kafirs was satisfying to the warrior, but it had an inherent problem: once everyone was killed, the warrior had to find other work. Mohammed therefore created the policy of dhimmitude to deal with the Jews. Dhimmitude was expanded later to include Christians, Magians, and others.

Dual ethics is at the very core of the concept of a dhimmi. Political subjugation of Kafirs can only come about by viewing them as separate and apart from Allah's true human beings, Muslims.

It can be argued that the glory of Islam came not from Islam but its dhimmis' wealth and knowledge. The dhimmis were the scholars, since the Arabs of Mohammed's day were barely literate and their classical literature was oral poetry. The secular knowledge of Islam came from the Christians, Persians, and Hindus.

Islam is credited with saving the knowledge of the Greeks from extinction. This is ironic in two ways. First, it was the jihad against the Byzantine/Greek culture that caused its collapse. Secondly, it was the Syrian Christian dhimmis who translated all of the Greek philosophers into Arabic.

The Hindu numbering system was credited to Islam. The Muslims took the zero from Hindu mathematicians, and today we call our numbers Arabic numerals. From carpets to architecture, the Muslims took the ideas of the dhimmis and obtained historical credit. The lists of great Islamic scholars includes the dhimmis with Arabic names living under Islamic dominance.

Over time, as the dhimmi population decreased, the "Golden Age" of Islam disappeared. There has never been a totally Islamic culture that was golden, brilliant or prosperous. Today there have only been eight Nobel prizes given to Muslims in the sciences. All of these were given for work done with Kafirs in Kafir countries. There has never been a scientific Nobel prize given for work in a Muslim country. For that matter, roughly half of all Arabs are illiterate.

Without the dhimmis, Islam is poor. The total economic output of all Arab countries (without the oil) is equal to that of Spain.

The dhimmis produced the wealth of Islam.

B4,53,388 Juwairiya said to Umar, "Oh, Caliph, give us your advice." Umar said, "You should continue the arrangement made by Mohammed regarding the dhimmis because the taxes they pay fund your children's future."

Dhimmitude is privation.

B4,53,380 Umar drove all the Kafirs from Arabia. After Mohammed conquered Khaybar, he considered expelling the Jews from the land of Allah, Mohammed and the Muslims. However, the Jews asked Mohammed if they could stay in exchange for their servitude and half of each harvest. Mohammed said, "You may stay on those terms as long as it pleases us." The Jews remained until Caliph Umar drove them from Arabia.

Dhimmitude means serving the Muslim masters.

B3,39,521 Mohammed made an agreement with the Jews of Khaybar that allowed them to use the land in exchange for half of each harvest. Mohammed would give each of his wives one hundred wasqs [a wasq is a camel-load], twenty wasqs of barley and eighty wasqs of dates. Upon becoming caliph, Umar gave Mohammed's wives the choice of continuing the practice, or assuming ownership of the land. Some wanted the land, while others chose the wasqs. Aisha wanted the land.

When Mohammed moved to Medina, half of Medina was Jewish. Less than two years later, two of the three tribes of Jews were exiled and their money and goods taken as spoils of war. The men of the third and last tribe were executed and their wives were taken as slaves of pleasure and domestic work; their children were raised as Muslims. Not one Jew was left in Medina.

After jihad comes dhimmitude: Jihad cracks open the culture; dhimmitude replaces it with Islam. Afghanistan was a Buddhist nation until conquered by Islam; Pakistan was Hindu; Egypt was the culture of the Pharaohs even though it had become Christian; and North Africa was Christian.

Today we locate cultures on continents, but up until 600 AD the Mediterranean Sea was the center of the map. Egypt was only a few days away from Italy, and Greek ships sailed into Egyptian harbors on a daily basis. Egypt and North Africa were much closer to the southern coast of the Mediterranean and European culture than they were African culture south of the Sahara. There was a Buddhist monastery in Alexandria, Egypt. The southern coast of the Mediterranean was once Roman, then became Christian. St. Augustine was from what is now called North Africa. Turkey was Christian and Buddhist. Iran (Persia) was Zoroastrian. The Hindu culture was twice as large as it is now.

Then came jihad, followed by dhimmitude. More than half of Christianity disappeared; half of Hindu culture disappeared; half of Buddhism was annihilated; Zoroastrianism disappeared. Languages were replaced by Arabic. The laws, customs, names, and history became extinct. When Napoleon invaded Egypt, he found that the Egyptian Arabs did not know anything about the pyramids or temples. Islam had annihilated even the memory of the pharaohs' 5,000-year-old culture.

So the progression was as follows: first jihad, then dhimmitude, and then the destruction of the native dhimmi culture. This became the model for the next 1400 years. The dhimmi became a second-class citizen in Islam and paid a heavy poll tax called the *jizya*. Only Jews and Christians and, sometimes, Magians (Zoroastrians) had the choice of becoming dhimmis. Buddhists, Hindus, and animists had the choice of death or conversion.

It was Umar II who set the standards for dhimmitude. His treaty with the dhimmis states:

> We shall not build, in our cities or in their neighborhood new monasteries, churches, convents, or monks' cells, nor shall we repair, by day or by night, such of them as fall in ruins or are situated in the quarters of the Muslims.
>
> We shall keep our gates wide open for passersby and travelers. We shall give board and lodging to all Muslims who pass our way for three days.

We shall not give shelter in our churches or in our dwellings to any spy nor hide him from the Muslims.

We shall not manifest our religion publicly nor convert anyone to it. We shall not prevent any of our kin from entering Islam if they wish it.

We shall show respect toward the Muslims, and we shall rise from our seats when they wish to sit.

We shall not seek to resemble the Muslims by imitating any of their garments.

We shall not mount on saddles, nor shall we gird swords nor bear any kind of arms nor carry them on our persons.

We shall not engrave Arabic inscriptions on our seals.

We shall not sell fermented drinks.

We shall clip the fronts of our heads (keep a short forelock as a sign of humiliation).

We shall always dress in the same way wherever we may be, and we shall bind the zunar round our waists.

We shall not display our crosses or our books in the roads or markets of the Muslims. We shall only use clappers in our churches very softly. We shall not raise our voices when following our dead. We shall not take slaves who have been allotted to Muslims.

We shall not build houses higher than the houses of the Muslims.

Whoever strikes a Muslim with deliberate intent shall forfeit the protection of this pact.

(from Al-Turtushi, *Siraj Al-Muluk*, p. 229-30)

But this excerpt can not really describe the world of the dhimmi. Islam dominated all public space. The government was Islamic; the education was Islamic; dress was Islamic; literature was Islamic. Only inside the dhimmi's house could there be no Islam. The word of a dhimmi could not be used in court against a Muslim and crimes against dhimmis were rarely prosecuted.

The wealth of Islam came from the wealth and labor of the subjugated dhimmis. This had been true ever since Mohammed sent out his first jihadists to raid a Meccan caravan. From that day onward, Islam became wealthy through violence against the Kafir. The perfect example of the Jews of Khaybar as dhimmis was used again and again. First jihad took the spoils of war and slaves; then the dhimmi tax system produced yearly wealth. Islam is a political system with a divine license to take what is wanted from *dar al harb*, the land of war.

These rules created a dhimmi culture throughout sixty percent of what had been Christian and European culture. Dhimmitude resulted in the total loss of the local culture.

2:193 *Fight them until you are no longer persecuted and the religion of Allah reigns absolute, but if they give up, then only fight the evil-doers.*

The treaty of Umar ensured that this was met.

The details of what happened varied from country to country. The Zoroastrian and Buddhist cultures collapsed under jihad and quickly disappeared. The Jews survived as the servants to Islam; some Christian cultures managed to exist for a thousand years before annihilation, and the Christians in other areas quickly became Muslims.

The actual attitude of Islam toward the dhimmis was more contempt than hatred, and over time the dhimmis disappeared. They either left or converted. It was too hard to be a second-class citizen, and the extra taxes were a burden. As time went on both Christians and Jews became more Arabic in their outlook; they started to treat women as the Arabs did and their customs became more and more Islamic. Finally it was easier to accept Islam as their religion and stop all the pressure and contempt.

This is the Sunna of Mohammed

BEHEADING

CHAPTER 5

*4:69 Those who obey Allah and His Messenger will live
with the messengers and the saints and the martyrs
and the righteous. What wonderful company!*

There are many references to beheadings in both the Sira and the Hadith. Many refer to the beheading of the Jews in Medina, the last of the three Medinan Jewish tribes.

Eight hundred male Jews were beheaded as Mohammed watched with his twelve-year-old wife.

B5,58,148 When some of the remaining Jews of Medina agreed to obey a verdict from Saad, Mohammed sent for him. He approached the Mosque riding a donkey and Mohammed said, "Stand up for your leader." Mohammed then said, "Saad, give these people your verdict." Saad replied, "Their soldiers should be beheaded and their women and children should become slaves." Mohammed, pleased with the verdict, said, "You have made a ruling that Allah or a king would approve of."

Here are a few of the references to beheadings.

M037,6676 Anas tells that a man was accused of having sex with a slave girl belonging to Mohammed. Mohammed said to Ali, "Chop off his head." Ali searched and found him cooling himself in a well. When Ali ordered him from the well, he discovered that the man had been castrated and refrained from decapitating the man. Ali returned to Mohammed and said, "The man cannot have had sex with your slave. He does not even have a penis." [The slave was black, since only black eunuchs had both the penis and testicles removed.]

Umar would behead his own daughter for Islam.

M009,3507 At the time Mohammed secluded himself from his wives, I [Umar B. Al-Khattab] went to the Mosque and discovered the people were very upset. They were saying, "Mohammed has divorced his wives." Of course, this was before men were ordered to avoid the contact of women at certain times. I thought to myself, "I need to discover what is going on."

I found Aisha and asked, "Have you made Mohammed mad?" She said. "Mind your own business." So I went to my daughter, Hafsa, and said, "People tell me that you have angered Mohammed. You realize that he doesn't love you and that if I wasn't your father he would already have divorced you." She began to cry and I asked. "Where is your husband, Mohammed?" "He is upstairs," she replied. I found Mohammed's black slave, Rabah, just outside the room and I called out, "May I speak with your Master?" Rabah looked in the room and then back at me without saying a word. I asked again, in a loud voice, "May I speak with Mohammed." Again, Rabah looked in the room and then at me and said nothing. Finally, I cried out very strongly, "I believe that Mohammed thinks I am here to intercede for my daughter, Hafsa. If he would say the word, I will cut off her head to please him."

M032,6255 While on an expedition with Mohammed, one of the immigrants tried to stab a man from the Helpers in the back. Both groups began to cry out and a large fight threatened to break out. Mohammed said, "What am I hearing? You people are acting like you did before Islam." Someone said, "Mohammed, an immigrant tried to attack a man from the Helpers while his back was turned." "That is disgraceful," Mohammed said. Abdullah B. Ubayy heard this and said, "It is true. When we get back to Medina, the Helpers will evict the immigrants." Umar then said, "Give me permission to cut off the hypocrite's head." Mohammed said, "No, no one can ever say that I kill my companions."

This is the Sunna of Mohammed

THE JEWS

CHAPTER 6

48:13 We have prepared a blazing Fire for these Kafirs
who do not believe in Allah and His Messenger.

In Islam's early days, Mohammed began to preach in Mecca where there were a few Jews and a handful of Christians. At first Mohammed's god had no name, but soon it was called Rahman and, then, Allah. There had been a moon god called Allah in Arabia since the dawn of time. Allah was the chief god of the Quraysh, Mohammed's tribe, and Mohammed's father was called Abdullah, slave of Allah. Mohammed said his was the only god and identified Allah with the One-God of the Jews, Jehovah.

Mohammed claimed to be the last in the line of Jewish prophets. The stories in the Koran resembled the Jews' stories of Adam, Moses, Noah, and other figures in Jewish tradition. The Meccans had a great deal of respect for the Jews because they had a sacred text. Indeed, both Jews and Christians were called People of the Book. None of the Arabian religions had a religious book as the native Arabic religions were tribal and based on oral traditions.

Then Mohammed went to Medina. Half of Medina was Jewish. Their leaders did not agree with Mohammed that he was a Jewish prophet. The revelations of the Koran took on a different tone about the Jews. Their scriptures did not agree with Mohammed's, therefore their scriptures were wrong. Clearly they had changed them to oppose Mohammed. Less than two years later, there were no Jews left in Medina, and the Muslims had their possessions.

DEMEANING HADITHS

B1,12,749 Mohammed: "Say Amen when the Imam says, 'not the path of those who anger You [the Jews] nor the path of those who go astray [the Christians]' everyone who says Amen will have their past sins forgiven."

> 1:1 *In the name of Allah, the Most Gracious, the Most Merciful*
> *In the Name of Allah, the Compassionate, the Merciful.*
> *Praise be to Allah, Lord of the worlds.*
> *The Compassionate, the Merciful. King of the Judgment Day.*
> *Only You do we worship, and to You alone do we ask for help.*

Keep us on the straight and narrow path.
The path of those that You favor; not the path of those who anger
You [the Jews] *nor the path of those who go astray* [the Christians].
[This sura is repeated every day by Muslims.]

B2,23,457 While walking after dark, Mohammed heard a mournful cry and said, "Jews are being punished in the afterlife."

B2,23,472 On his deathbed, Mohammed said, "The Jews and the Christians are cursed by Allah because they build houses of worship over the graves of their prophets." If this had not been revealed, Mohammed's tomb would have been a shrine. As it was, Mohammed, and the people, were afraid that his grave would become a holy site for worshiping Allah.

Mohammed claimed the mantle of all the Jewish prophets. He claimed that Allah was Jehovah and that all religious truth came through Allah. Islam has the best claim to Moses.

B3,31,222 After coming to Medina, Mohammed witnessed the Jews observing a fast on the day of Ashura. Asked about that, they said, "This is a holy day. It celebrates the day God delivered the Jews from their enemy. Moses fasted this day." Mohammed told them, "Muslims have more right to claim Moses as a prophet than you do." Consequently, Mohammed fasted that day and required all Muslims to fast on that day.

Jews lie.

B3,41,599 Mohammed said anyone who lies under oath with the aim to illegally take a Muslim's property will face Allah's wrath. Al-AshAth said, "That statement pertained to me. A Jew and I shared some common land, and he had denied that I was co-owner of the property. I took the dispute before Mohammed, who asked if I had proof of ownership. I said that I did not. Mohammed then asked the Jew to swear an oath that he was the rightful owner of the land. I said, "Mohammed, he will swear a false oath and steal my land." Therefore, Allah revealed this verse to Mohammed:

> 3:77 *Those who sell their covenant with Allah and their oaths for a meager price will have no part in the world to come.*

B4,56,662 Mohammed said, "You will imitate the sinful behavior of your ancestors so utterly and completely that if they did something stupid, you would do exactly the same thing."

We asked, "Are you talking about the Jews and the Christians?"

He answered, "Who else could I be talking about but the Jews and the Christians?"

B4,56,664 Aisha despised the practice of praying with hands on the flanks because that was the way the Jews used to pray.

B4,56,668 Mohammed: "When the head of a Jew or a Christian becomes gray, they refuse to dye their hair. You must do the opposite of their behavior. Therefore, dye your hair and beard when they become gray."

B6,60,157 Mohammed: "May Allah curse the Jews! Allah ordered them to not eat animal fat, so what do they do? They melt it down, sell it, and invest the proceeds."

B6,60,252 Musab: "I questioned my father about this certain verse, specifically if it pertained to breaking a pledge."

18:103 *Say: Shall We tell you whose actions will make them the biggest losers?*

"He said, 'No, it pertains to the Jews and the Christians. The Jews did not believe Mohammed, and the Christians did not believe in Paradise and said that there is no eating or drinking there. People who make and confirm pledges to Allah and then break them, reject obedience to Allah and are evildoers.'"

Jews are the cause of decay and rebellious wives.

B4,55,547 Mohammed: "If it weren't for the Jews, meat would not rot. If not for Eve, wives would never disobey their mates."

B2,23,376 As Mohammed walked past a weeping family of Jews at their daughter's funeral, he said, "They are crying for her and she is being tortured in the grave."

JEWS ARE FALSE; ISLAM IS THE TRUTH

Islam is pure and true. The Jews and their scriptures are corrupt and untrue, and the same is true of Christians and their scripture.

B3,48,850 Ibn Abbas: "Muslims, why do you ask the Jews or Christians anything? The Koran, revealed directly to Mohammed, is the most-up-to date instruction that we have from Allah. You recite it word for word, and it is not modified. Allah tells you that the Jews and Christians have taken it upon themselves to change the word. They claim that their altered Scriptures are from God, but they make that boast to gain material rewards in this world. Hasn't enough been revealed to you through Mohammed to stop you from asking them anything? I never see any of them asking you about your revelations."

M003,0592 It was the practice of the Jews to refrain from eating with or being with menstruating women. Mohammed's companions asked him about this, and so Allah revealed to him an answer:

> 2:222 *They ask you about women's menstrual cycle. Say: It is a discomfort. Therefore, keep away from them during this time and do not come near them until they are clean again.*

Mohammed said, "Normal contact is permissible, just don't have sex during menstruation."

When the Jews heard what Mohammed instructed, they said, "Mohammed will oppose anything we say or do."

Usaid B. Hudair and Abad B. Bishr went to Mohammed and told him what the Jews said. They concluded that they should follow the example of the Jews and avoid any contact with menstruating women. It appeared at first that Mohammed was angry with the two men, but later they were given a quantity of milk as a gift and forwarded it to Mohammed. Mohammed had them brought to him, gave them something to drink, and let it be known that he was not angry with them.

B6,60,91 Marwan told his gatekeeper, Rafi, to find Ibn Abbas, and tell him. "If everyone who takes joy in their actions, likes to be praised for the things they do not do, then everyone will be punished." Ibn Abbas said, "What does this have to do with you? It concerns a matter whereby Mohammed asked the Jews about something, and they obscured the truth, by dissembling. They felt like they deserved praise for responding to his question, but at the same time, they felt pleasure at hiding the full truth. Then Ibn Abbas recited:

> 3:187 *When Allah entered into a covenant with those to whom the Scripture had been given He said, "Make these Scriptures known to mankind and do not hide them," but they threw them behind their backs and sold them for a meager price! [Mohammed said that the original Torah predicted his coming. The Jews corrupted their scriptures to conceal his prophecy.] Their exchange was evil. Do not think that those who exult in their sins and love to be praised for what they have not done will escape their punishment.*

Jews will swear a false oath.

B8,73,164 Abdullah and Muhaiyisa traveled to Khaybar, and while walking in the gardens among the date-palms, Abdullah was murdered. Abdur-Rahman, Huwaiyisa and Muhaiyisa went to Mohammed and told him of their friend's murder. Mohammed said "Will fifty of you swear an oath naming the culprit and giving yourselves the right to the blood money associated with his wrongful death?" They responded, "We did not witness the murder." Mohammed said, "The Jews can release you from your oath if fifty of their number should swear an oath that contradicts your own." They said, "They are Kafirs. They will merely make a false oath." Mohammed agreed and paid the men the blood money out of his own pocket.

B6,60,79 A man and woman charged with adultery were brought before Mohammed by the Jews. Mohammed asked them, "How are adulterers usually punished ?" They said, "We blacken their faces with coal and beat them." Mohammed said, "Doesn't the Torah order them to be stoned to death?" They answered, "We do not find that in the Torah." Abdullah, overhearing the conversation, said, "You lie. Bring the Torah and recite the relevant passage if you are telling the truth."

When a Torah was brought before Mohammed, a rabbi began to read from the book, but obscured the relevant passage with his hand. Abdullah saw this and removed the man's hand from the book and asked, "What verse is this?" They answered, "The verse regarding stoning." Mohammed then ordered the man and woman to be stoned to death. As the sentence was being carried out, I saw the man attempt to shield the woman from the stones with his body.

M037,6666 Mohammed: "Allah will use a Christian or Jew to substitute for a Muslim in Hell."

Some rats are changed Jews.

M042,7135 Mohammed: "A tribe of Bani Isra'il [Jews] disappeared. I do not know what became of them, but I think they mutated and became rats. Have you noticed that a rat won't drink camel's milk, but it will drink goat's milk?"

Everyone is born a Muslim.

M033,6423 Mohammed: "The nature of humans at birth is Allah's choice. Everyone is born a Muslim. A child is made a Jew or a Christian by his parents, just as an animal creates an offspring that looks just like itself. Is any defect apparent?" Mohammed then quoted the Koran:

> 30:30 *Set your resolve as a true convert to the religion that Allah has created, and for which He has created man. Allah's creation can not be changed. This is the right religion, but most people do not know.*

JIHAD

This hadith marks the formal break with the Jews and sets the stage for jihad against them. Until this time, Mohammed and his followers faced Jerusalem when praying.

B1,8,392 For approximately a year and a half, Mohammed faced Jerusalem while praying, but he preferred to face the Kabah in Mecca, so Allah revealed:

> 2:144 *We have seen you [Mohammed] turn your face to every part of Heaven for guidance, and now We will have you turn to a Kiblah [the direction faced during prayer] that pleases you.*

Therefore, Mohammed faced Mecca to pray and the foolish Jews said, "Why have you stopped facing Jerusalem while praying?"

Allah revealed:

> 2:142 *Say, Both the east and the west belong to Allah. He will guide whom He likes to the right path.*

A man, after praying with Mohammed facing Mecca, went forth and told the people, "I testify that I prayed with Mohammed facing Mecca." Soon everyone faced Mecca while praying.

The next hadith marks the beginning of religious apartheid in Arabia. To this day there are no churches, temples, or synagogues in Arabia.

B3,39,531 Umar drove the Christians and the Jews from Arabia. Mohammed defeated the Jews at Khaybar and gave ownership of the land to Allah, the Muslims, and Mohammed. But now Umar wished to evict the Jews. The Jews, however, asked to remain on the condition that they provide the labor to sustain the city and in return they would receive half of the proceeds. Mohammed said, "You may stay under those conditions until we change our minds." They remained in Arabia until Umar expelled them from the land.

Jews are the enemy of Islam.

B3,50,890 After Abdullah was attacked by some citizens of Khaybar, Umar gave a sermon and announced, "There is no dispute that Mohammed made an arrangement with the Jews of Khaybar regarding their property there. However, Abdullah was recently attacked in the night while visiting his land, his feet and hands injured. The Jews are our enemies, our only enemies in Khaybar and the only suspects. Therefore, I have decided to expel them."

After Umar announced his decision, one of Abu's sons spoke to him. "Umar, as chief of the Muslims, will you expel us from our land despite the agreement we made with Mohammed which permitted us to remain in exchange for our labor and a half share of the return?"

Umar retorted, "Do you think that I do not remember Mohammed asking your people, 'How do you think you will be doing when you are expelled from the land, riding your camel for many days and nights?' Abu's son said, "Mohammed was jesting." Umar replied, "Jew, enemy of Allah, you are a liar." Umar then expelled all the Jews, compensating them for their possessions with dry goods, food, tools and cash.

B5,59,366 To commemorate Mohammed's burning of the Jews' date-palm trees, Hassan wrote a poetic verse in Arabic:

"The dreadful arson of Al-Buwaira is ignored by the privileged, the rulers and nobility of Quaraysh."

Abu Sufyan, a cousin of Mohammed who had not yet converted to Islam, answered Hassan in poetic verse.

"May Allah smile upon that fire and may he engulf all of Medina in flames. The light it casts will illuminate those far away (Al-Buwaira) and those near in Medina."

Al-Ashraf, a Jew, wrote a poem criticizing Islam. The only critics of Mohammed who lived did so by converting to Islam.

B5,59,369 Mohammed said, "Who will murder Al-Ashraf, the man who insults Allah and Mohammed His prophet?"

Bin Maslama said, "Mohammed, will it make you happy if I kill him?"

Mohammed said, "Yes." Bin Maslama then said, "Give me permission to lie to him, so that he will not suspect my scheme."

Mohammed replied, "You may deceive him to achieve our goal."

Bin Maslama went to Al-Ashraf and said, "Mohammed threatens us and demands more taxes. Can you loan me some food?"

Al-Ashraf said, "I said that you would get sick of him and tired of him."

Mohammed Bin Maslama replied, "He is our leader, and we don't want to desert him before we know how things are going to turn out. For now, we just want to borrow a couple of camel- loads of food."

Al-Ashraf said, "Certainly, but you have to give me some collateral."

Mohammed Bin Maslama asked, "What do you want?"

"Your women," Al-Ashraf replied.

"We can't do that, you are the best looking Arab there is," Mohammed Bin Maslama replied.

"All right, how about your sons?" Al-Ashraf asked.

"No. We can't do that either. People would mock them for being ransomed for a camel load of food. We will mortgage our weapons for the food."

Mohammed Bin Maslama and Al-Ashraf's foster brother, Abu Na'ila, soon returned at night seeking entry into Al-Ashraf's fort. As he was preparing to let them in, Al-Ashraf's wife asked, "Who is it?"

He replied, "It is merely Mohammed Bin Maslama and my foster brother, Abu Na'ila."

She said, "Don't let them in, his voice drips with blood."

"I know these men. Even if it is an invitation to death, a generous man should answer a call at night," Al-Ashraf said.

After entering, Bin Maslama said to his companions, "When Al-Ashraf comes in, I will touch and smell his hair. I will ease his suspicions by appealing to his vanity, by asking him to allow you to smell his hair. When you see that I have a strong grip on him, strike quickly." Kab-Bin Al-Ashraf entered the room dressed and smelling strongly of perfume.

Mohammed Bin Maslama complimented him, saying, "What is that aroma? I have never smelled anything so good."

Al-Ashraf said, "I employ the best Arab women to make my perfumes."

Mohammed Bin Maslama said, "Let me smell your hair." Al-Ashraf agreed and allowed Bin Maslama and then his companions to smell his hair.

When Bin Maslama was granted permission to smell Al-Ashraf's hair a second time, he grabbed Al-Ashraf's head and yelled to his accomplices, "Get him!" The men quickly struck Al-Ashraf down, and they hurriedly left and reported to Mohammed. Abu Rafi was murdered soon after Al-Ashraf.

Assassination, stealth, and deceit were used by Mohammed to eliminate his Jewish opposition.

B5,59,371 Mohammed sent several Medinan converts, under the leadership of Abdullah to kill Abu Rafi, a Jew who opposed Mohammed and aided the struggle against him. Abdullah and the other assassins approached Abu Rafi's castle in Hijaz at night just as the townspeople were bringing their animals in for the night.

Abdullah told his accomplices, "Stay here. I'll try to get in by fooling the guard."

Abdullah covered his armor and weapons with a cloak and eased close to the gate. Pausing, he pretended to urinate, causing the gate-keeper to believe he was merely a servant from the castle finishing his business before entering the castle.

The guard said to him, "Hurry up. I have to close the gate."

Abdullah described it like this:

I entered the castle and found a place to hide. After the last person had entered the city and the guard had left, I grabbed the keys from a peg where the guard had left them. I unlocked the gate and began to sneak upstairs where Abu Rafi was entertaining guests. To avoid detection, I closed each door behind me after entering. I thought to myself, even if his guards find out I'm here, they will never be able to catch me before I kill him. He was sleeping in a dark apartment, surrounded by his family and I could not identify him. So, I called, "Abu Rafi."

He answered, "Who is it?"

I followed the sound of his voice and stabbed him with my sword. Because of the darkness, I did not deliver a mortal blow and he cried out in pain and alarm. I slipped out of the room for a moment before returning and posing as a concerned neighbor.

I said, "What's wrong, Abu Rafi?"

He replied, "An intruder has attacked me."

I then stabbed him in the stomach, killing him. I stumbled about in the dark trying to escape. Falling down, I hurt my leg before reaching the city gate, where I rested and awaited confirmation that Abu Rafi was dead, determined not to leave the city with him alive. At daybreak, a town crier announced that Abu Rafi was dead.

I rejoined my companions saying, "Let's get out of here before we are killed. Allah has slain Abu Rafi." We rode away and immediately informed Mohammed about the death of his enemy.

He listened to our report and said, "Abdullah, let me take a look at your hurt leg." He massaged it, and it was healed as if it was never injured.

Two of the Jewish tribes of Medina had been exiled and their property taken. This hadith marks the death knell of the remaining Jews. All the men were killed; the women became slaves, and the children were raised as Muslims. An interesting sidelight is that the Jews of Arabia had a rare genetic disease. Today that disease is found in the Arab descendents of those Jews in Arabia.

B5,59,448 During the battle of the Trench, Saad was badly wounded in the arm by an arrow shot by Hibban, a Quraysh. Mohammed erected a tent for Saad in the Mosque and visited him frequently. Pausing from the battle, Mohammed returned to his tent, removed his weapons and bathed. As he was shaking the dust from his hair, the Angel Gabriel revealed himself to Mohammed and said, "Have you quit the fight?"

Mohammed said, "No."

Gabriel replied, "Then attack them."

Mohammed asked, "Where should I attack?"

Gabriel pointed to the Jews. Mohammed then returned to battle and besieged the Jews who soon surrendered and put themselves in Mohammed's hands. Mohammed, however, gave the decision regarding their fate to Saad, who declared, "It is my judgment that their men be killed, their property confiscated, and their women and children enslaved."

According to Hisham, his father told him that he heard Aisha say, "Saad said, 'Allah, you know that I love nothing more than to wage jihad against your enemies. I believe that you have now ended our struggle against the Quraysh. However, if there remains any fighting to be done between us, allow me to live and rejoin the fight against them. If, on the other hand, our battle with them has ended, let me die of my wounds right now. Blood immediately began to gush from the wound and streamed out of the tent, alarming those nearby.'"

Women as the spoils of war.

B5,59,512 During the night, just outside Khaybar, Mohammed gave the Fajr Prayer and said, "Allah is great! Khaybar will be in ruins. When we attack a city that has been warned, those people are in for an evil morning." As the people of Khaybar fled the city, Mohammed ordered the men killed and the women and children enslaved.

Safiya was amongst the captives. She first was the slave of Dihya but later on she belonged to Mohammed. Mohammed made the price of her freedom her wedding dowry.

B5,59,522 After the fall of Khaybar, people told Mohammed about a beautiful Jewess named Safiya, whose husband had been slain by Mohammed when she was still a newlywed. [In addition, he had her father tortured to death and killed her cousin.]

Mohammed claimed Safiya for himself and took her away. After Safiya's menstrual cycle ended, Mohammed married her. He gave her his knee to stand on so she could climb up on to his camel, and he made a pillow for her out of his cloak so she might ride behind him.

To be protected from Islam, the Jew must submit to Islam.

B9,92,447 We were at the Mosque one day when Mohammed came out and said, "Let's go talk to the Jews."

When we arrived at their village, Mohammed addressed them saying, "Jews, submit to Allah. Become Muslim and you will be protected."

They answered, "You have delivered Allah's word, Mohammed."

Mohammed said, "That is my wish, accept Islam and you will be protected."

They repeated, "You have delivered Allah's word."

Mohammed said for a third time, "That is my wish; accept Islam and you will be protected," before adding, "You need to know that the Earth belongs to Allah, and I intend to expel you from this land. If you have property, you should sell it; otherwise, you had better remember that this land belongs to Allah and Mohammed."

B4,52,68 During the battle of the Trench, Mohammed paused from fighting, stripped off his weapons, and bathed. Gabriel, covered in dust, revealed himself to Mohammed and said, "You have laid down your weapons. I have not laid my arms down yet."

Mohammed asked, "Where do you want me to go?"

Gabriel said, "That way," pointing toward the Jewish camp.

Mohammed armed himself and marched into battle.

When the Jews of Fadak heard what had happened to the Jews of Khaybar, they surrendered before they were even attacked by Mohammed.

B4,52,153 Because the property of the Jews that Allah had given to Mohammed had not been won by the Muslims through the use of their horses and camels, it belonged exclusively to Mohammed. Mohammed used it to give his family their yearly allowance and he spent the rest on weapons and horses for jihad.

THE JEWS AS DHIMMIS

What is important about these hadiths is that they established the relationship between Islam and the Jews. The Jews were the first dhimmis, and that was their only relationship with Islam for 1400 years until the establishment of Israel in 1947.

The image one usually has of the Jews in Islam's golden era is that they were respected and honored scholars functioning at a high level in society. The court physician was a Jew, and Jews were among the wise councilors who served the caliph or sultan. There is some truth in this image, but the Jews were never a threat to Islam as they had no real political power. Having no real political power, they were not as persecuted as the Christians were.

However, given the dual nature of Islam, this golden picture had vast exceptions. All the rules of a dhimmi fell on the Jew as well as the Christian. In North Africa, the Jews did all the unclean work: they cleaned the cesspools and were tanners, butchers, and hangmen. They even had the task of drying the sewage from the cesspools for sale as fuel. The Jew was inferior; the Muslim was superior.

A Muslim must not massage a Jew or a Christian nor throw away his refuse nor clean his latrines. The Jew and the Christian are better fitted for such trades, since they are the trades of those who are vile. A Muslim should not attend to the animal of a Jew or of a Christian, nor serve him as a muleteer, nor hold his stirrup. If any Muslim is known to do this, he should be denounced.[1]

Any time a Jew rose too high in rank in the government, there was always the chance he would be brought down.

QUESTION: A Jew has been appointed inspector of coins in the treasury of the Muslims to weigh the dirhams (gold coins) that come and go and to test them, and his word is relied upon in this. Is his appointment permissible under the Holy Law or not? Will God reward the ruler if he dismisses him and replaces him with a competent Muslim? Will anyone who helps to procure his dismissal also be rewarded by God?

ANSWER: It is not permissible to appoint the Jew to such a post, leave him in it, or to rely on his word in any matter relating to this. The ruler, may God grant him success, will be rewarded for dismissing him and replacing him with a competent Muslim, and anyone who helps to procure his dismissal will also be rewarded. God said,

> 3:118 Believers! Do not become friends with anyone except your own people. The Kafirs will not rest until they have corrupted you. They wish nothing but your ruin. Their hatred of you is made clear by their words, but even greater hatred is hidden within their hearts. We have made Our signs clear to you. Therefore, do your best to comprehend them.

The meaning of this is that you should not adopt outsiders, that is, Kafirs, and allow them to penetrate to your innermost affairs.[2]

Humiliation and contempt were an important part of the ethic in relating to Jews. The favorite epitaph for a Jew was the one Mohammed used, "apes." Christians were called "pigs." Dhimmis were never to have higher status than Muslims.

QUESTION: If a ruler prevents the dhimmis who live among the Muslims from building high and ornamented houses, riding horses inside the city, dressing themselves in sumptuous and costly garments, wearing kaftans with collars and fine muslin and furs and turbans, in sum from deliberate actions to belittle the Muslims and exalt themselves, will that ruler be rewarded and recompensed by God?

ANSWER: Yes. The dhimmis must be distinguished from the Muslims by their dress, their mounts, their saddles, and their headgear.[3]

---

1. Ibn Abdun, *Risala fil-qadq wal-hisba*, ed. E. Levi-Provencal (Cairo, 1955), 43ff.
2. Bernard Lewis, *The Jews of Islam* (Princeton, N.J.: Princeton University Press, 1984), 29-30.
3. Paul Horster, *Zur Anwendung des islamischen Rechts im 16. Jahrhundert* (Stuttgart, 1935), 37.

And again:

And whereas, in reply to this, my imperial decree had already previously been written and sent, concerning the dress of the Kafirs. Therefore I now command that when this present arrives, you proceed in accordance with my previously sent imperial decree and ensure that henceforth neither Jew nor Christian nor any other Kafir be allowed to wear fine clothes, as set forth above, and in contravention of my previously issued noble command.

(Given to the Inspector of Markets)

15 August 1568.[4]

And it was not wise for a Jew to enter into any theological discussions about Islam. Here is a comment about the Jews in Egypt by Edward Lane:

At present, they are less oppressed; but still they scarcely ever dare to utter a word of abuse when reviled or beaten unjustly by the meanest Arab or Turk; for many a Jew has been put to death upon a false and malicious accusation of uttering disrespectful words against the Koran or the Prophet.[5]

This treatment was for all People of the Book, Jews and Christians. This scene is from Turkey in 1908:

The attitude of the Moslems towards the Christians and Jews, to whom as stated above, they are in a majority of ten to one, is that of a master towards slaves whom he treats with a certain lordly tolerance so long as they keep their place. Any sign of pretension to equality is promptly repressed. It is often noticed in the street that almost any Christian submissively makes way even for a Moslem child. Only a few days ago the writer saw two respectable-looking, middle-aged Jews walking in a garden. A small Moslem boy, who could not have been more than eight years old, passed by and, as he did so, picked up a large stone and threw it at them—and then another—with the utmost nonchalance, just as a small boy elsewhere might aim at a dog or bird. The Jews stopped and avoided the aim, which was a good one, but made no further protest.[6]

Islam could treat the dhimmi Jews in one of two ways, both equally acceptable. They could be physicians in the court of the caliph or they could

---

2. Ahmed Refik, *Onuncu asr-I hicride Istanbul hayati* (Istanbul, 1333), 68-9.

5. Edward William Lane, *An Account of the Manners and Customs of the Modern Egyptians*, 5th ed. (London, 1871), 305.

6. H.E. Wilkie Young, "Notes on the City of Mosul," enclosed with dispatch no. 4, Mosul, January 28, 1909, in F.O. 195/2308; published in *Middle Eastern Studies* 7 (1971): 232.

be "apes" at which a small boy tossed a rock. Both roles are supported by the Koran of Mecca and the Koran of Medina, continuing the dualistic nature of Islam.

This is the Sunna of Mohammed

CHRISTIANS

CHAPTER 7

*4:115 Anyone who opposes the Messenger after having
received Our guidance and follows a path other than
that of the true believer will be left to their own devices.
We will lead them into Hell, an evil home.*

The Koran says that Christians who submit to Islam can go to Paradise. Every reference to Christians in the Hadith is negative.

A Muslim repeats the following sura daily:

*1:1 In the name of Allah, the Most Gracious, the Most Merciful In
the Name of Allah, the Compassionate, the Merciful.
Praise be to Allah, Lord of the worlds. The Compassionate, the
Merciful. King of the Judgment Day.*

*1:5 Only You do we worship, and to You alone do we ask for help.
Keep us on the straight and narrow path. The path of those that
You favor; not the path of those who anger You [the Jews] nor the
path of those who go astray [the Christians].*

B1,12,749 Mohammed: "Say Amen when the Imam guides you along the right path and says, 'not the path of the Jews who deserve your anger, nor the way of the Christians who have gone astray.' All of a Muslim's past sins are forgiven when they say Amen in concert with the angels."

B2,23,472 On his deathbed, Mohammed said, "Allah has cursed the Jews and Christians because they have built churches and temples over the graves of their prophets." If he had not said that, Mohammed's grave would have been a prominent focal point for Muslims. Evidently, Mohammed, or the people, were afraid that his grave might be mistaken for a place of worship.

The Christians and Jews who reject Mohammed will go to Hell.

M001,0284 Mohammed: "According to Allah, any Jew or Christian that is aware of me, but dies before accepting my prophecy will be sent to Hell."

Religious apartheid in Arabia.

B3,39,531 Upon the death of Mohammed, Umar drove the Jews and Christians out of Arabia. Mohammed had intended to do so after he had conquered Khaybar, as the land then became the possession of Allah, Mohammed, and the Muslims. Mohammed granted their request to remain, however, in exchange for their labor and half of the proceeds. Mohammed said, "You may stay under those conditions for as long as we allow it." Thus they remained until Umar expelled them from Arabia.

B4,56,662 Mohammed warned the people, "You will follow the errant path of those who came before you so completely, that if they did a stupid thing, you would too." The people asked, "Mohammed, do you mean the Christians and the Jews?" He answered, "Whom else would I mean?"

The very earth rejects those who criticize Islam and Mohammed.

B4,56,814 Once there was a Christian who accepted Islam, studied the Koran, and wrote down Allah's revelations to Mohammed. The man later reverted back to Christianity and would say, "Mohammed doesn't know anything except what I have written down for him."

After the man died and was buried, his friends found his body disinterred. They said, "This is the work of Mohammed and his followers. They have pulled him from his grave because he rejected them."

The man's friends dug another, deeper grave and reburied their friend. The next day, however, the man's body was again found thrown from the grave.

His friends again blamed Mohammed and his companions for the act and proceeded to dig another, even deeper grave.

In the morning, the man's friends again found the grave empty and the body thrown on the ground. The man's friends were then convinced that the earth had rejected the man's body and that humans were not to blame, so they left the body on the ground.

M033,6423 Mohammed: "No one is born that is not created according to his true nature. A parent turns his child into a Jew, Christian, or pagan, just as an animal produces an offspring that imitates itself." He then quoted the Koran, "Allah creates man according to his natural state. There can be no alteration by man to what Allah has created. This natural state is the correct religion."

M037,6666 Mohammed: "Allah will fill a Muslim's place in Hell with a Christian or a Jew."

B6,60,252 Musab asked his father, "Does this verse pertain to people who break their pledges?"

> 18:103 *Say: Shall We tell you whose actions will make them the biggest losers?*

His father said, "No, it refers to the Jews and the Christians. The Jews did not believe in Mohammed and the Christians did not believe in Paradise, saying that there is not food or drink there." Saad called them practitioners of evil that reject obedience to Allah.

B7,67,387 Abu Tha'laba said, "Mohammed, we live in a land ruled by Jews. Is it permitted to eat using their utensils? Game is plentiful there and I hunt with my bow and with a trained and an untrained hound. Am I permitted to eat such game as I take in such a manner?"

Mohammed said, "Regarding the people of the Scripture that rule your land, don't eat from their utensils if you can get your own. If you cannot get your own utensils, then you may eat from theirs after they are washed. If you first invoke Allah's name, you may eat game you kill with your bow. If you first invoke Allah's name, you may eat the game taken with your trained hound. You may also eat game taken with your untrained hound if you slaughter the game before it dies."

When Christians submit to Islam, their ethics can be good.

B8,76,504 Mohammed related to us two parables, one pertains to events that I [Hudhaifa] have witnessed, and the other to events yet to come.

Mohammed said that in the beginning, honesty was ingrained in the hearts of men. Later it was learned from the Koran and the Traditions of Mohammed. He then related how honesty would disappear, saying, "Man will go to sleep and honesty will be stolen from his heart, leaving only a trace, such as a fire will leave behind. Man will again fall asleep and the remaining honesty in his heart will be taken away, leaving only a trace that resembles a blister that contains nothing. The moral of the story is that a day will come when people will not be trustworthy in business dealings. An honest man will then be pointed to as an exception, rather than an example. Then a man will be praised for his strength, intelligence and character, even though his faith is as small as a mustard seed."

Hudhaifa continued: "Formerly, I was not concerned about doing business with anybody. A Muslim's faith would prevent his dishonesty, and a Christian's Muslim ruler would compel his honesty. Today, I will do business with only a few people."

Mohammed said, "By Him in Whose Hands my soul is, Jesus will shortly descend amongst you Muslims as a just ruler and will break the

Cross and kill the pig and abolish the tax taken from the Kafirs. Then there will be abundance of money and nobody will accept charitable gifts."
Christ will return.

B3,34,425 Mohammed: "According to Allah, Jesus will soon appear to Muslims as a fair and equitable ruler. He will shatter the cross and slay the swine and cancel the tax levied on Kafirs. Then there will be plenty of money and none will require charity."

Muslims believe the Christian scriptures were corrupted to conceal the truth about the superior religion of Islam and Mohammed's superiority to Christ.

B3, 48, 850 Ibn Abbas: "Muslims, why do you ask the Jews and Christians any questions? The Koran that was revealed to Mohammed contains the latest word from Allah. It has not been altered and you recite it daily. Allah has made clear to you that the Jews and the Christians have distorted the Scriptures that were revealed to them. They have claimed that their alterations are the word of God in order to achieve some material gain."

This is the Sunna of Mohammed

SLAVES

CHAPTER 8

*4:42 On that day the Kafirs and those who disobeyed
the Messenger will wish they could sink into the earth
for they cannot hide a single thing from Allah.*

Islam has a complete set of laws concerning slavery. Here are some of
the hadiths that form the basis of these Islamic laws. The ethical system
of slavery is pure dual ethics.

RULES, REGULATIONS

B1,3,97 Mohammed: "Three classes of people will be doubly rewarded
in Paradise:

A Jew or a Christian who formerly believed in Jesus or Moses, but
then accepted Islam and believed in Mohammed.

Slaves who fulfill their obligations to their masters and Allah.

The owner of a slave-woman who teaches her proper etiquette, in-
doctrinates her in the ways of Islam, and then grants her freedom and
marries her."

Here we can see the application of the second point.

Teyeb (an escaped African slave): We were taught that to escape is lit-
erally to go against the commands of Allah, for the Bedyane [Bedouins,
Muslim Arabs] teach us that slavery is one of Allah's sacred principles.
"The way to Paradise is under your master's feet," they said.[1]

The good treatment of a slave includes beatings.

B7,62,132 Mohammed: "Nobody should beat his wife as he would a
slave and then have sex with her that night."

M001,0131 Mohammed: "If a slave flees his master, Allah does not
hear his prayer."

---

1.   Interview with Moctar Teyeb, "Slavery Is a State of Mind," *Middle East
Quarterly* 6 (December 1999):.

B2,25,579 Mohammed set a charity tax rate of six pounds of dates or barley on every Muslim slave or free-person, male or female, young or old, and demanded it be paid before the people made the Id prayer.

B3,34,299 My father purchased a slave who produced income by bleeding patients (cupping) to treat their ills, but he soon smashed the slave's instruments. I [Aun] asked him why he did that, and he said Mohammed decreed that no one should be paid money for a dog or for blood. He also banned giving or getting tattoos, giving or demanding excessive rates of interest, and he put a curse upon painters of images.

B3,34,315 Abu bled Mohammed and in return Mohammed instructed that he be given six pounds of dates and decreed that his owners reduce his slave tax. (Abu was a slave and therefore required to pay a special tax.)

B3,34,362 Mohammed: "If it is proven that a slave girl has had illegal sex, her master should whip her but should not continue to fault her after she is punished. If it should again be proved that she had illegal sex, her master should whip her but should not fault her after the legal punishment. If she should commit the infraction for a third time, he should sell her for even the smallest price."

B3,46,710 Utba asked his brother Saad to care for his illegitimate son who was born to Zama's slave girl. Saad, accompanied by Abu, brought the boy before Mohammed when he was in Mecca for the fall of that city. Saad said, "Mohammed. This is Utba's son. He has made me the boy's guardian."

Abu then said, "Mohammed, that boy is my brother. His mother is Zama's slave-girl and he was born on my father's bed."

Mohammed looked at the boy and saw the resemblance to Utba. Mohammed said to Abu, "The boy is in your care because he is also your father's son." Mohammed then told his wife, Sauda, to wear her veil in the boy's presence because his resemblance to Utba was unmistakable. (His paternity saved him from being a slave like his mother.)

B3,46,723 Mohammed: "Any man that educates his slave girl, teaches her etiquette, grants her freedom, and then marries her will receive a double reward in Paradise. Any slave that accepts Allah's and his owner's mastery will be doubly rewarded in Paradise."

B3,48,827 Uqba married a woman named Um Yahya. He said, "A black slave woman came to me and said, 'I wet-nursed you and your wife.'" I told Mohammed about this and he turned his head. I walked around and looked him in the face and he said, "How can you remain married to Um Yahya when you know that you both suckled at the same breast?" Mohammed ordered Uqba to divorce Um Yahya.

B9,83,42e: Umar asked the advice of Mohammed's companions regarding a woman who lost a child through an unwanted abortion caused by another person. Al-Mughlra said, "Mohammed said that either a male or female slave should be awarded as compensation." Mohammed Bin Maslama corroborated the story.

B3,36,483 Mohammed banned the practice of using slave girls as prostitutes.

B3,46,702 Ibn Umar gave similar verdicts in disputes centering on slaves owned by more than one master, where one owner wished to free the slave from his share of bondage. In cases like that Umar would say, "The slave owner who wishes to free a slave from his share of bondage should completely free the slave if he has the resources to fairly compensate the other owner(s). The other owners should accept the fair price and free the slave."

SLAVES IN THE DAILY LIFE OF ISLAM

Slaves are as common as camels in the Hadith, Sira, and Koran. Here are some selections that show the ubiquity of slaves in everyday life.

B2,15,103 During the days of Mina, Abu Bakr visited Aisha. While Mohammed was lying down, two young slave girls were beating a tambourine. Abu Bakr yelled at them to stop their noise. Mohammed uncovered his face and told Abu Bakr, "Leave them alone. It's the days of 'Id and the days of Mina [festival days]."

Aisha also said, "One time Mohammed was hiding me from public view so that I might watch some black slaves in the Mosque display their skill with weapons.

Umar scolded them for exhibiting themselves in the presence of a Muslim woman, but Mohammed said, "Leave them alone. You Negroes may continue; you have my protection."

B3,27,22 Asma's slave Abdullah once told me that he could hear Asma when she would walk by Al-Hajun. She would say, "May Allah bless His messenger Mohammed."

B3,38,500 We used to graze sheep at Sala. One time, one of our slave-girls saw a dying sheep. She chipped a rock and used it to kill and butcher the animal. My father told everyone, "Don't eat that meat until I speak to Mohammed." My father asked Mohammed if the meat was permissible to eat, and he said that it was. Ubaidullah said, "I admire that girl. Even though she is a slave, she had the courage to slaughter that sheep."

B3,47,743 Mohammed sent for an Immigrant woman who owned a slave skilled in carpentry. Mohammed said to her, "Order your slave to build a pulpit." She did so, and he built a pulpit of tamarisk wood. Upon completion, it was brought to Mohammed who personally lifted and situated the pulpit where you now see it.

B5,58,262 The first Muslims to emigrate from Mecca to Medina were Mus'ab and Ibn Um Maktum, who taught the Koran to the Helpers. Next came Umar and twenty other followers of Mohammed. When Mohammed came to Medina, he said, "I had never seen the people so happy. Even the slave girls were shouting, 'Mohammed is here!'"

B8,73,229 Mohammed was traveling one time and slave called Anjasha was urging the camels to run faster. Mohammed said, "Anjasha, drive the camels with the fine glassware more slowly." By fine glassware, he meant the female passengers.

MOHAMMED AND SLAVERY

Islam has the most developed religious attitude, legal framework, social theory, and customs regarding slavery. The term *slave* is a positive one in Islam. Mohammed referred to himself and Muslims as the "slaves of Allah." Mohammed's second convert was a slave.

Mohammed himself was involved in every single aspect of slavery. He had non-believing men killed so that the surviving women and children could be made slaves[1]; he owned many slaves, some of them black,[2] and he gave slaves away for gifts;[3] he passed around slaves for the purpose of sex to men who were his chief lieutenants.[4] Mohammed stood by while others beat slaves;[5] he captured slaves and wholesaled them to raise money for jihad.[6] He shared the pleasure of sex with the captured women after conquest.[7] One of his favorite sexual partners was a slave

---

1. Guillaume, *Life of Mohammed*, 466.
2. Ibid., 516.
3. Ibid., 499.
4. Ibid., 593.
5. Ibid., 295.
6. Ibid., 466.
7. Ibid, 496.

who bore him a son.[8] He got slaves as gifts from other rulers.[9] The very pulpit that he preached from was made by a slave.[10] He ate food prepared by slaves.[11] He was treated medically by a slave[12]. Mohammed had a slave tailor[13]. He declared that a slave who ran away from his master would not have his prayers answered.[14] He approved an owner's having sex with his slaves.[15] He called himself a slave of Allah.

THE BLESSING OF SLAVERY

In the Koran the word *slave* is frequently used for followers of Allah. The Koran usually calls slaves "captives of the right hand" (the sword hand), and Arabic has at least eight words for slaves.

To a Muslim, slavery was a blessing for all concerned, including the slave. It merely reflected the natural order of Allah's universe and was Allah's way of bringing Islam to the slave. Mohammed, the ideal human pattern, showed that slavery was part of the sacrament of jihad, which produced slaves. If at some point in the life of the slave or the slave's descendants they converted to Islam, slavery was a manifest blessing. Islam proclaimed that a slave was to be treated well, and one of the highest acts of a Muslim was to free a slave.

WHITE SLAVES

For 1400 years—until the slave market was officially closed in the early 1960s—the highest priced slave in Mecca was the white woman. The price of a white slave girl was from three to ten times that of a black girl. When Islam invaded Spain, the first thing exported back to Islamic North Africa was a thousand blond-haired girls.

Our word for slave comes from the Slavs of eastern Europe. So many of them were taken by the Muslims of the Ottoman Empire that the very term *Slav* came to mean slave. And black slaves were so numerous that the term *abd* came to mean black or African. Muslims called the white slaves *mamluk*.

---

8. William Muir, *The Life of Mohammed* (New York: AMS Press, 1975), 425.
9. Ibid.
10. Bukhari, Hadith, Volume 1, Book 8, Number 440.
11. Ibid., Volume 3, Book 34, Number 295.
12. Ibid., Volume 3, Book 36, Number 481.
13. Ibid., Volume 7, Book 65, Number 344.
14. Muslim, Hadith, Book 001, Number 0131.
15. Ibid., Book 008, Number 3383.

Not only were the words for slaves different but the uses of them were different. The white woman was favored for sex. That is why she brought the best price. White slaves were not used for rough labor but were used for higher positions in domestic and administrative work. Both white and black men were used as eunuchs in the harem.

Both white and black male slaves were used in the armies of Islam; however, whites could become officers, governors, and rulers. Advancement happened only rarely for blacks. Only one black slave rose to the rank of ruler: Abu I Misk Kafur was a eunuch and became a governor of Egypt.

In Eastern Europe, the Islamic rulers taxed the Christian families at the rate of one fifth; one child in five was taken for slavery. These children were forcibly converted to Islam and trained to form the core of the *janissaries*, the military troops used by the Turkish sultan. The sultan reserved younger children for the palace, where they were trained by the eunuchs for positions in the administration of the Islamic empire. This theft took place annually among the Greeks, Serbs, Bulgarians, Albanians, and Armenians. At a fixed date, each father had to appear in the town square for the sultan's man to come pick the best of his children for Islam.

The strategy ensured that the population of Muslims increased and the population of Christians decreased.

When the Serbs revolted against Islamic oppression and were crushed in 1813, eighteen hundred women and children were sold in one day to Muslims in Belgrade.[1] During the Greek revolt against Islamic rule, the Islamic ruler sent four to five thousand rebels to be sold in Constantinople and thirty-four hundred women to be sold as slaves.[2]

In the seventeenth century, Jean de Chardin wrote:

> Shah Abbas I transported settlements of twenty or thirty thousand souls at a time, two or three hundred leagues from their native land. Almost all of them were Georgian and Armenian Christians [...] It was in this way that the kings of Persia rose to that point of absolute power which I will show, and which they sustain [...] because as almost all the Georgians and Iberians [from South Caucasus region] who are given the status to govern are slaves by origin, and genuine outsiders in the government, they have no contacts either in the kingdom or with one another. As most of them know neither from where nor from whom they come, it happens that they are not driven by any desire

1. Castellan, *Histoire des Balkans*, 254
2. Broughton, *Travels,* letter written May 11, 1825 by Jean-Bafriel Eynard.

for freedom on the one hand and are incapable of forming leagues or conspiracies on the other. Men who have no relationship among themselves do not rise in rebellion on behalf of each other, either to save their lives or to ascend the throne.

This name of *coular* means slave, not that these men are not as free as other Persians, but because they are natives of countries such as Georgia, Circassia, Iberia, and of Moscow, from where slaves are drawn. Thus they are of Christian origin. Some were sent to the king as gifts, being still young; others are descended from the peoples of these countries, who have become accustomed to Persia. As almost all of them embrace the Islamic religion, they are all renegades or the children of renegades.[3]

BLACK SLAVES

In theory, the races are equal in Islam, but they have not always been so in practice. Long before Islam, the Arabs had enslaved blacks. After Islamic expansion, the Islamic empire needed more slaves so they came from the traditional source, Africa. Massive importation of illiterate people performing hard labor did not enhance the Muslim view of blacks, no matter how vital they had been in Mohammed's day. Here is one caliph's opinion of the black slave he received as a gift:

> Had you been able to find a smaller number than one and a worse color than black you would have sent that as a gift.[4]

And another opinion:

> Therefore, the Negro nations are, as a rule, submissive to slavery because Negroes have little that is essentially human and have attributes that are quite similar to those of dumb animals, as we have stated.[5]

The major exploitation of black slaves took place outside the cities. Since Islam is primarily an urban culture, it is the urban culture recorded in its writings. Therefore, we don't know much about the lives of the rural slaves. The picture we have of Islamic slavery is that of the palace, the army, and domestic workers.

Large gangs of slaves were used for heavy construction, agriculture, mining, and dredging operations. Large landowners would employ

---

3. Jean de Chardin, *Voyages du Chevalier de Chardin En Perse*, Paris, 1811, 5226-28, 306-8
4. Jahsihari, *Kitab Al-Wuzara wa l-Kuttab* (Cairo, 1938), p. 81
5. Translated by F. Rosenthal, Ibn Khaldun, *The Muqaddimah*, vol. 1 (New York, 1958), p. 301

thousands of black slaves for agricultural work. Urban slaves performing administrative and domestic work had relatively light duty, but
those performing manual labor led a brutal life. The slaves, mainly men,
who worked the Saharan salt mines lasted an average of five years before
death. Slave women were used as prostitutes, although the practice was
explicitly forbidden by the Koran.

Over time, there has been a great deal of discussion about the enslavement of Muslim blacks. Islamic law about this was very clear;
any Kafir could be enslaved after jihad, but no Muslim, black or any
other, was to be enslaved. To resolve the matter, one simply disputed
the devoutness of the slave's faith and concluded he or she was "not
really Muslim."

The Muslims of north Africa captured so many of their black brothers
that there was a body of legal rulings, *fatwas*, on the subject. The fatwas
concluded that the benefit of the doubt went to the owner, not the slave.[1]
There was an immediate outcry from black Muslim rulers, decrying the
jihad launched against their subjects, and their black jurists protested
the enslavement of Muslims, but the practice continued.[2]

Enslavement went hand in hand with death. Not only were family
members killed protecting their loved ones, but many others died on the
relentless march from their villages of capture. Only the best humans
were taken; thus, villages were left under-populated with the young,
weak, sick, and very old. Starvation, disease, and heartbreak destroyed
those who remained. One author of the nineteenth century estimated
that, for every slave on the auction block, nine others died.[3]

Here is a quote from David Livingstone about the aftermath of slave
trading in Africa:

> Now as the exploring party ascended the river the desolation was
> heart-breaking. Corpses floated past them in such numbers that the
> paddle-wheels had to be cleared from them every morning. Wherever
> we took a walk, human skeletons were seen in every direction, and it
> was painfully interesting to observe the different postures in which
> the poor wretches had breathed their last. Many had ended their
> misery under shady trees, others under projecting crags in the hills,
> while others lay in their huts with closed doors, which when opened
> disclosed the moldering corpse with the poor rags around the loins,

---

1. Amad Al-Wansharisi, *Kitab Al-Miyar Al-mughrib*, vol. 9 (1895-96), 71-72
2. EII, s.v. "Abd" (by r. Brunschvig), p.32a; Rotter, *Die Stellung des Negers*,
44, 49ff.
3. Hourst, *Mission hydorgraphique du Niger*, 1896.

the skull fallen off the pillow, the little skeleton of the child, that had perished first, rolled up in a mat between two large skeletons. The sight of this desert, but eighteen months ago a well peopled valley, now literally strewn with human bones, forced the conviction upon us that the destruction of human life in the middle passage, however great, constitutes but a small portion of the waste, and made us feel that unless the slave-trade—that monster inequity, which has so long brooded over Africa—is put down, awful commerce cannot be established.[4]

And why did the killing and slaving take place?

We had a long discussion about the slave trade. The Arabs have told the chief that "our object in capturing slaves is to get them into our own possession and make them of our own religion."[5]

And what was the emotional impact on the survivors?

The strangest disease I have seen in this country seems really to be broken-heartedness, and it attacks Kafir men who have been captured and made slaves. Speaking with many who died from it, they ascribed their only pain to the heart, and placed the hand correctly on the spot, though many think that the organ stands high up under the breast-bone. Some slavers expressed surprise to me that they should die, seeing they had plenty to eat and no work. It seems to be really broken hearts of which they die.[6]

Islamic slavery was the basis of all the slavery in the West. When the white slaver arrived in his boat on the coast of Africa, he went to see a Muslim trader. The New World was a new market for the ancient Islamic slave trade. The only change was the boat and the direction it sailed. Two hundred years went by before the Atlantic slave trade was stopped. But it never has stopped in Islam.

SEX SLAVES

The Koran and Hadith are very clear on the subject of sex and slaves in Islam. Sex with the slave is sanctioned by the following verse. It is wrong for a Muslim to have sex with another Muslim's wife but not with married slaves and captives. This is dual ethics.

---

4. J.H. Worcester: The Life of David Livingstone. Woman's Presbyterian Board of Missions of the Northwest. Chicago. 1888, 59-60.
5. Ibid. 62.
6. Ibid.

4:24 Also forbidden to you are married women unless they are your slaves. *This is the command of Allah. Other than those mentioned, all other women are lawful to you to court with your wealth and with honorable intentions, not with lust. And give those you have slept with a dowry, as it is your duty. But after you have fulfilled your duty, it is not an offense to make additional agreements among you. Truly Allah is knowing and wise!*

The great Islamic geographer, Al-Idris, was of the opinion that Nubian women made the best slaves of pleasure.

Their women are of surpassing beauty. They are circumcised and fragrant-smelling...their lips are thin, their mouths small and their hair flowing. Of all black women, they are the best for the pleasures of the bed...It is on account of these qualities of theirs that the rulers of Egypt were so desirous of them and outbid others to purchase them, afterwards fathering children from them.[1]

By the early nineteenth century the taste in slaves for sex (concubines) had changed to Ethiopian (Abyssinian) women, at least in Mecca.

There are few families at Mecca, in moderate circumstances, that do not keep slaves...the concubines are always Abyssinian slaves. Wealthy Mekkawys [Meccans] do not prefer domestic peace over the gratification of their passions; they keep mistresses in common with their lawful wives...Many Mekkawys have no other than Abyssinian wives, finding the Arabians more expensive, and less disposed to yield to the will of the husband...The same practice is adopted by many foreigners, who reside in the Hijaz for a short time. Upon their arrival, they buy a female companion, with the design of selling her at their departure; but sometimes their stay is protracted; the slave bears a child; they marry her, and become stationary in the town. There are very few unmarried men, or those without a slave. This, indeed, is general in the East, and no where more so than at Mecca.[2]

When wealthy Muslims had enough money, they preferred white sex slaves. A white female slave was about three times more expensive than an Ethiopian woman.

The white female slaves are mostly in the possession of wealthy Turks. The concubine slaves in the houses of Egyptians of the higher

---

1. J. O. Hunwick, "Black Africans in the Islamic World: An Understudied, Dimension of the Black Diaspora," *Tarikh 5* (1978), no. 4:27.
2. John Lewis Burckhardt, *Travels in Arabia, vol. 1* (London:1829), 340-42.

and middle classes are, generally, what are termed "Habasheeyehs," that is, Abyssinians.[3]

There is one more aspect of sexual slavery involving mutilation: the eunuchs. The removal of a man's sex organs made him socially available to all women, even in the harem. From the Koran:

> 24:31 *And tell the women who are believers that they should lower their eyes and guard their purity, and they should not display their beauty and adornments except that which is normally shown. They should cover their breasts with their veils and only show their adornments to their husband, father-in-law, sons, step-sons, brothers, nephews, or their female servants, eunuch slaves, and children who are innocent and do not notice a woman's nakedness. And do not let them stamp their feet so as to reveal their hidden adornments [ankle bracelets]. Believers, all of you turn to Allah and repent so that it will go well for you.*

Since Islamic prohibitions would not allow Muslims to castrate slaves, they chose to pay a higher price for slaves castrated in *dar al harb*, [outside of Islamic territory] not *dar al Islam*.

There is a fascinating aspect of Islamic castration: white male slaves had only their testicles removed. Blacks lost both testicles and penis. Black eunuchs were traditionally used for the attendants of the Mosque of the Prophet in Medina.

MODERN SLAVERY

Enslavement of blacks by Muslims continues to this day in Africa. The two most active sites of modern slavery are the Sudan and Mauritania.

So the duality of slavery in Islam is its claim on the one hand to treat its slaves well and expose them to Islam, while, on the other hand, subduing a population of people into slavery with extreme violence.

BLACKS

Blacks are mentioned in passing in the hadiths, usually in a negative tone. Mohammed frequently used the term *raisin head* for Ethiopians and Africans.

B1,11,662 Mohammed: "Obey and listen to your ruler, even if he is an Ethiopian with a head like a raisin."

---

3. E. W. Lane, *An Account of the Manners and Customs of the Modern Egyptians,* 5th ed., vol. 1 (London: 1871), 168-169, 233-34.

B2,15,70 One time when Mohammed was in my [Aisha's] house, two slave girls were singing songs commemorating some old battles in the days before Islam. Mohammed had lain down facing away from me and the two girls, when Abu Bakr entered the house and began to scold me saying, "You allow Satan's music around Mohammed?" Mohammed turned around to Abu Bakr and said, "Leave them alone."

I soon told the girls to leave. Outside black soldiers were displaying their skill with spear and shield. Either I asked to watch the display, or Mohammed asked me if I wished to see it, but in any event Mohammed had me stand behind him, our faces together, cheek to cheek. He called out, "Carry on, Negroes." When I tired of the display, Mohammed asked if I had seen enough. When I replied that I had, he told me to leave.

Blacks will do evil in the future to Islam.

B2,26,661 Mohammed: "An Ethiopian with two skinny legs will destroy the Kabah."

B9,87,163 Mohammed: "In a dream I saw a black woman with messy hair leaving Medina to live in Mahaia. I think that it meant that an epidemic would begin in Medina and would be spread to Mahaia."

B4,52,309 My [Rafi's] grandfather asked Mohammed, "We may engage the enemy tomorrow, but we have no knives. How shall we slaughter our animals?"

Mohammed answered, "If you invoke Allah's name beforehand and you use a tool that causes profuse bleeding, then you may eat. However, do not use a tooth or a nail to slaughter an animal. A tooth is the same as a bone, and it is forbidden to slaughter with a bone. You should not use a nail because that is what the Ethiopians (Africans) use, and we don't want to copy them."

This is the Sunna of Mohammed

WOMEN

CHAPTER 9

3:131 *Obey Allah and His messenger so
that you may receive mercy.*

There are many references in the Hadith to women and their place in
the world.

HELL

Most of those in Hell will be women.

B1,2,28 Mohammed said, "I have seen the fires of Hell and most of its
residents are ungrateful women." He was asked, "Are they Kafirs, or did
they show ingratitude to Allah?" He answered, "They were not grateful
to their husbands and not grateful for the kindness shown them."

Women are inferior to men in intelligence and religion.

B1,6,301 While on his way to pray, Mohammed passed a group of
women and he said, "Ladies, give to charities and donate money to the
unfortunate, because I have witnessed that most of the people in Hell
are women.

They asked, "Why is that?"

He answered, "You swear too much, and you show no gratitude to your
husbands. I have never come across anyone more lacking in intelligence,
or ignorant of their religion than women. A careful and intelligent man
could be misled by many of you."

They responded, "What exactly are we lacking in intelligence or faith?"

Mohammed said, "Is it not true that the testimony of one man is the
equal to the testimony of two women?"

After they affirmed that this was true, Mohammed said, "That illustrates that women are lacking in intelligence. Is it not also true that
women may not pray nor fast during their menstrual cycle?" They said
that this was also true.

Mohammed then said, "That illustrates that women are lacking in
their religion."

Women are ingrates.

B2,18,161 During the life of Mohammed, there was a solar eclipse. Mohammed gave the special eclipse prayer and stood upright for a long time. He then alternately bowed and stood for long periods of time before prostrating himself and finishing the prayer. When he had finished, the eclipse had ended.

Mohammed said, "The moon and the sun are two signs of Allah. They are not eclipsed because of the birth or death of someone. When you look at them, think of Allah."

Some people said, "Mohammed, we saw you reach out to something and then retreat."

Mohammed answered, "I witnessed Paradise, and I reached out my hand toward some wonderful fruit that grows there. If I had been able to return with that fruit, you might have eaten it until the end of time. I also witnessed the fires of Hell. Never have I seen such a dreadful sight. Furthermore, most of the people there were female."

The people wondered, "Why was that?"

Mohammed responded, "Because of their ingratitude." When he was asked if it was because they were ungrateful to Allah, Mohammed said, "No, it is because of their ingratitude toward their husbands and for their ingratitude for the good things they were blessed with. You could be kind and benevolent to a woman all of her life, but if she sees one fault in you, she will say, 'You have never been good to me.'"

SEX

B1,3,132 Um Sulaim went to Mohammed and said, "Obviously, Allah does not hesitate to tell you the true nature of things. If a woman has a wet dream, must she take a bath afterwards?" Mohammed said, "Yes, if she is aware of it." Um Sulaim shielded her face and asked Mohammed, "Do women have wet dreams?" "Yes," he answered. "Why do you try to contradict me? It is no wonder that the son acts like the mother."

M008,3367 Mohammed: "If a man wishes to bed his wife and she refuses, Allah will be displeased with her until her husband is pleased with her."

The man gets exile and one hundred lashes for adultery; the woman is killed.

B3,49,860 A nomad and another man came before Mohammed, seeking his solution to a dispute.

The nomad said, "Mohammed, use Islamic law to settle our dispute." The other man said, "Yes, we will abide by Allah's law as you dictate."

The nomad began, "My son worked for this man and he fornicated with the man's wife. Some people said that he must be stoned to death; to save him from that punishment, I paid a penalty of one hundred sheep and one slave girl. Then I asked some Islamic scholars who said, "Your son must be given one-hundred lashes and be exiled one year.""

Mohammed said, "I will settle this dispute using Allah's law. Your son must be exiled for one year, and he must be lashed one hundred times. The slave-girl and the one hundred sheep will be returned to you." Mohammed then turned to a companion and said, "Unais, seize this man's wife. She must be stoned to death." Consequently, Unais went and stoned the woman to death.

CLEAN/UNCLEAN

B1,4,227 A woman asked Mohammed, "If a woman gets menstrual blood on her clothes, what should she do?" He answered, "She should rub it in cold water to remove the stain and then rinse the garment well. She may then wear the garment when praying."

B1,4,228 Fatima asked Mohammed, "My uterus bleeds persistently. I can't remain clean. Must I forsake praying?" Mohammed said, "No. The bleeding is caused by blood vessels, not your menses. When your cycle begins, refrain from prayer. When the cycle is over, take a bath and resume prayers."

B1,6,295 Someone asked Urwa, "May a menstruating woman serve me? Is it permissible for a menstruating woman to come close to me?" I answered, "That is an easy question. They may serve me, and it will do no harm if they serve anybody else. Aisha told me that she would comb Mohammed's hair when she was menstruating, and he was in the Mosque at the time."

B1,8,347 During the two Id festivals, we were told to bring out our menstruating and veiled women from religious services and invocations. Specifically they were to be kept from their prayer rugs. A woman asked Mohammed, "What about the women that do not have a veil? Mohammed said, "Let her share the veil of a friend."

INFERIOR STATUS

B2,20,192 Mohammed: "A woman should not travel for more than three days unless accompanied by her husband, or a man whom she cannot marry, like her father, brother, or grandfather."

M031,5966 Mohammed: "There are many perfect men, but the only perfect women are Mary, the daughter of Imran, Asiya, the wife of Pharaoh, and Aisha (Mohammed's favorite wife). The superiority of Aisha to other women is like comparing Tharid [an unknown reference] to other foods."

B2,20,194 Mohammed: "A woman who believes in Allah and the Day of Reckoning may not travel for more than one day unaccompanied by a close male relative."

M036,6603 Mohammed: "After I am gone, the biggest threat to stability that will remain is the harm done to men by women."

B3,31,172 Mohammed: "Is it not a fact that women do not pray or fast during menstruation? That is the deficiency in her religion."

B6,60,51 The Jews used to have an old saying, "If during sex you enter your wife from behind, then your child will have squinty eyes." Consequently, Allah revealed this verse to Mohammed:

> 2:223 *Your women are your plowed fields: go into your fields when you like, but do some good deed beforehand and fear Allah. Keep in mind that you will meet Him. Give good news to the believers.*

B3,44,674 Aisha was asked whether she and Mohammed had discussed a certain Koranic verse. She responded, "Oh nephew, That verse concerns an orphan girl that lives with her male guardian and shares his possessions. Her good looks and wealth might persuade him to marry her without giving her a suitable dowry which she might get from another man. Therefore such marriages are forbidden if an adequate dowry is not provided." Aisha continued, "People still asked Mohammed about marrying orphan girls after that verse was revealed, so Allah revealed these verses:

> 4:127 *When they ask your advice regarding women say: Allah has instructed you concerning them, and His will is laid out for you in the Scriptures concerning female orphans to whom you have not given their legal due but whom you refuse to marry."*

B3,48,826 Mohammed asked, "Is not the value of a woman's eye-witness testimony half that of a man's?" A woman said, "Yes." He said, "That is because a woman's mind is deficient."

B7,62,31 Mohammed: "If anything can be a bad sign, it would be a house, a horse, or a woman."

B7,62,33 Mohammed: "After I die, the biggest problem that I leave to man is woman."

B7,62,113 Mohammed: "A woman is like a rib; if you try to straighten her out, she will break. To get any benefit from her, you must leave her crooked."

B7,62,123 Mohammed: "It is unlawful for a woman, while her husband is home, to fast without his permission. Furthermore, she must not let anyone enter his house without his permission. If she gives away any of his money to charities without his permission, he will get half the reward in Paradise."

Old age of women is a reason for divorce in Islam. When one of Mohammed's wives turned forty she made an arrangement to stay in Mohammed's harem because his wives were guaranteed Paradise, but she gave up sex.

B7,62,134 Concerning the verse:

> 4:128 *And if a wife fears cruelty or desertion from her husband, then they are not to blame for coming to a mutual agreement between themselves, for peace is best, although people are often prone to greed.*

Allah's statement pertains to the man who wishes to divorce his wife and marry another. His wife asks him not to divorce her, but rather keep her without any compulsion to have sex with her or provide for her.

An abused, beaten, and bruised woman appeared in front of Mohammed.

B7,72,715 Upon her divorce from Rifaa, a woman married Abdur Rahman. Soon after she went to Aisha, wearing a green veil, and complained of her new husband's brutality, showing her the discolored bruises on her skin.

Aisha interceded on her behalf with Mohammed saying, "I have never witnessed women being mistreated as much as Muslim women. Look at her bruises. She has been beaten greener than the veil she wears."

When Abdur Rahman learned that his new wife had complained to Mohammed about his behavior, he went to the prophet accompanied by his two sons from a previous marriage. His wife said, "I have done this man no wrong. Furthermore, he is impotent and as good to me as this floppy fringe that hangs from my robe."

Abdur Rahman responded, "She lies. I am very virile and can satisfy her, but she doesn't obey me and she wants to remarry Rifaa."

Mohammed told the woman, "If that is your wish, you should know that is illegal for you to remarry Rifaa if you have not had sex with Abdur

Rahman. Mohammed then looked to the two boys accompanying Abdur Rahman and asked, "Are these your boys?"

Abdur Rahman said, "Yes."

Mohammed then said to the woman, "You say he is impotent? Those boys look just like him."

Mohammed made no comment about her beaten and bruised face to her or to her husband. In his last sermon in Mecca he condoned lightly beating women.

CREATURES OF PLEASURE

Kafir women are for the pleasure of Muslim men, and forced sex with captives is approved.

B5,59,459 Entering the Mosque, Ibn Muhairiz saw Abu Said and asked him whether coitus interruptus is sanctified by Allah.

Abu Said said, "Accompanying Mohammed at the battle of Banu Al-Mustaliq, we were rewarded with Arab captives, including several woman who were very sought-after because celibacy had become quite a hardship. We had planned to practice *coitus interruptus* [when sold as slaves later, the women would bring a lesser price if pregnant] but felt that we should seek instruction first from Mohammed.

Mohammed said, however, "It is better that you not interrupt copulation to prevent pregnancy because if a soul is predestined to exist, then it will exist."

MARRIAGE

The most important part of a woman is her vagina.

B7,62,81 Mohammed said, "The marriage vow most rightly expected to be obeyed is the husband's right to enjoy the wife's vagina."

B7,62,121 Mohammed: "If a woman refuses her husband's request for sex, the angels will curse her through the night."

B7,62,140 The example of Mohammed dictates that if a man has an older woman as a wife and then marries a virgin, he should stay with the virgin for a week. If a man has a virgin wife and then marries an older woman, he should stay with her for three days.

It is the custom of Islam to shave the pubic area.

B7,62,173 Mohammed said, "If you return home after an absence, do not rejoin your family until your woman has had a chance to shave her pubic hair and get her hair done." Mohammed also said, "Jabir, make some babies!"

B7,62,16 While returning from jihad with Mohammed, I [Jabir] began to drive my lazy camel very hard. A rider behind me spurred my mount with a prick from his spear, and it began to run as fast as any of the others. Looking back, I saw that the rider in question was Mohammed.

He asked me, "Why are you in such a hurry?"

I answered, "I am a newlywed."

He asked, "Did you marry a older woman or a virgin?"

I said, " An older woman."

Mohammed asked, "Why did you not marry a young nubile girl? They are more playful."

As we approached Medina, Mohammed said, "Wait until tonight to enter the city. This will give the unkempt woman a chance to comb her hair and the woman whose husband has been away the opportunity to shave her pubic hair."

TEMPORARY MARRIAGE

A unique custom of Islam is temporary marriage. For an amount of money, a man can sleep with a woman for three days. Shia Islam still has this custom.

B7,62,51 Abu Jamra witnessed Ibn Abbas deliver a verdict permitting temporary marriages between jihadists and eligible women. Upon hearing this verdict, a freed slave of Ibn Abbas asked, "This is only permitted if it is really necessary and woman are hard to come by, correct?"

Ibn Abbas replied, "Yes."

B7,62,52 Jabir and Salama were fighting against the Kafirs when Mohammed went to them and said, "You are permitted to relieve yourselves by temporarily marrying. You should take advantage of the opportunity. If a man and woman agree to such a union it should last for three nights. They may continue the union or separate as they please after the third night."

I did not know if this arrangement was specific to us or if it pertained to all Muslims.

Later, Abu Abdullah (Al-Bukhari) related that Ali insisted that Mohammed said, "The temporary marriage arrangement has been cancelled."

B7,62,130 Abdullah said, "While on jihad with Mohammed, many of us did not have wives accompanying us. We asked whether we should get castrated?" Mohammed ordered us not to do that, and he gave us permission to take temporary wives before reciting this verse.

> 5:87 *O, you who believe, do not forbid the good things that Allah allows you, but do not commit excess for Allah does not love those who commit excess.*

M008,3248 We went to Jibir B. Abdullah's home when he came to perform Umra. There the people asked him about many things, among them the temporary marriage. He said, "Yes, we have enjoyed the temporary marriage while Mohammed was alive and also during the reigns of Abu Bakr and Umar."

M008,3252 Mohammed gave us permission to take a temporary wife. Another man and I [Sabra Juhanni] saw a very attractive Bana Amir woman, so we approached her with our marriage offers. She asked us what sort of dowry we could offer. I offered my cloak, as did my companion. Now, my companion's cloak was better than mine, but I was younger and better looking than he was. Finally, she said to me, "You and your cloak are good enough for me." She and I stayed together for three nights when Mohammed said that any of us with temporary wives should allow them to go.

RULES

B7,63,259 Mohammed cursed the female tattoo artist and the tattooed woman, the woman that either gives or receives excessive interest. He forbade selling dogs for a price, earning money through prostitution, and he cursed painters of pictures.

B7,72,815 Allah's curse is on women that either give or receive tattoos; those that pluck their facial hair and those that do anything to alter their natural appearance. If such actions are cursed by Allah and Mohammed, why should I presume to treat such women differently? This is revealed in the Koran:

> 59:7 ...*take what the Messenger has offered you, and refuse what he has forbidden you. And fear Allah, for Allah is severe in His punishment.*

B7,62,133 A woman from the Helpers had a daughter whose hair began to fall out soon after she became wed. The woman asked Mohammed his advice saying, "My daughter's husband suggests that she wear a wig." Mohammed said, "Don't let her do that. Allah curses women who wear artificial hair."

B3,38,508 Mohammed said, "Unais, confront this man's wife and if she admits committing adultery have her stoned to death."

B8,82,803 Ali had a woman stoned to death on a Friday and said, "I have punished her as Mohammed would have."

B7,62,159 Mohammed said, "Men should beware entering a woman's abode." One of the Helpers asked, "Even a woman's male in-laws?" Mohammed said, "A woman's in-laws should be particularly wary."

MISCELLANEOUS

B3,38,505r A woman said to Mohammed, "I want to give myself up to you." A man then asked, "If she is yours, will you give her in marriage to me?" Mohammed said, "With what you know of the Koran, we will marry her to you."

B4,52,43 Aisha said, "Mohammed, women believe that jihad is the most righteous act. Shouldn't women fight in jihad?" Mohammed replied, "Hajj [pilgrimage to Mecca], in the tradition of Mohammed, is the best act that a woman can perform. It is acceptable to Allah."

M003,058 Mohammed's wife Maimuna relates: When I menstruated, Mohammed and I would lie together with a cloth separating us.

One of Islam's greatest theologians was Al Ghazali, the equivalent of Christianity's St. Thomas Aquinas. He best summarized the state of women in his *Counsel for Kings*:

As for the distinctive characteristics with which God on High has punished women, the matter is as follows:

When Eve disobeyed Almighty God and ate fruit which He had forbidden to her from the tree in Paradise, the Lord, be He praised, punished women with eighteen things:

(i) menstruation;

(ii) childbirth;

(iii) separation from mother and father and marriage to a stranger;

(iv) pregnancy through him;

(v) having no control over her own person;

(vi) having a lesser share in inheritance;

(vii) her liability for being divorced and her inability to divorce;

(viii) it is lawful for men to have four wives, but for a woman to have only one husband;

(ix) the fact that she must stay secluded in the house;

(x) the fact that she must keep her head covered inside the house;

(xi) (the fact that) two women's testimonies have to be set against the testimony of one man;

(xii) the fact that she must not go out of the house unless accompanied by a near relative;

(xiii) the fact that men take part in Friday and Feast Day prayers and funerals while women do not;

(xiv) disqualification for rulership and judgeship;

(xv) the fact that merit has one thousand components, only one of which is attributable to women, while nine hundred and ninety nine are attributable to men;

(xvi) the fact that if women are profligate, they will be given only half as much torment as the rest of the Muslim community at the Resurrection Day;

(xvii) the fact that if their husbands die, they must observe a waiting period of four months and ten days before remarrying;

(xviii) the fact that if their husbands divorce them, they must observe a waiting period of three months or three menstruation periods before remarrying.[1]

Islam has dual ethics for the female and the male.

This is the Sunna of Mohammed

---

1. Al-Ghazali, *Counsel for Kings*, translated F. R. C. Bagley (Oxford University Press, 1964) 164-65.

SEX

CHAPTER 10

8:20 Believers! Be obedient to Allah and His messenger, and
do not turn your backs now that you know the truth. Do
not be like the ones who say, "We hear," but do not obey.

RULES ABOUT SEX

B1,4,143 Mohammed: "If, before having sex with his wife, a man says, 'In the name of Allah, shield us from Satan and protect the off-spring of our union from Satan.' Then if it is ordained that a child should be conceived, Satan will be powerless to harm that child."

B1,4,179 I [Zaid Bin Khalid] consulted Uthman about a man who had sex, but did not ejaculate. Uthman answered, "He should perform the regular prayer purification ritual, but he must also clean his penis." Uthman said, "Mohammed told me this." Others whom I asked about this said the same thing. (This was later rescinded, and an order that a bath be taken was substituted instead.)

M002,0566 After staying the night in Aisha's home, a man washed his clothes after waking. Aisha told him, "If you saw some semen, washing the spot would serve to purify the garment. If the spot was not visible, then sprinkling water around it would suffice. When I see semen on Mohammed's clothes, I merely scrape it off and he says a prayer while getting dressed."

B1,5,269 Formerly, I [Ali] would have occasions where I would have a non-sexual ejaculation. Since Mohammed was my father-in-law, I asked someone to consult him about my problem. Mohammed told him, "Perform the purification ritual after washing your penis."

B1,5,280 Um Sulaim, Abu Talha's wife, went to Mohammed and asked, "Mohammed, obviously, Allah does not shrink from speaking the truth to you. Must a woman bathe after having a wet dream?" Mohammed answered, "Yes, if she had a discharge."

B1,5,290 Mohammed: "When a man is encompassed by a woman and has had sex with her, a ritual bath is necessary."

B8,74,312 Mohammed: "There are five things that prophets have in common: circumcision, shaved pubic hair, plucked armpits, a closely trimmed moustache, and trimmed finger nails."

B3,44,683 Mohammed and some followers arrived at Mecca one morning. Later when our group arrived, Mohammed ordered us to change our plans regarding the consecration of an upcoming lesser pilgrimage. He said that we could go home to our wives for sex and that we could complete our consecration after the lesser pilgrimage. This stirred up the people. Jabir, gesticulating, asked with evident surprise, "Are we to go to the holy valley with semen dripping from our penises?"

Mohammed heard of the commotion, and after giving a sermon said, "I have been told that some of you were up in arms. By Allah, I am more afraid of Allah than any of you. I am more obedient to his will than any of you. If I had known then what I know now, I would have left the sacrifice with you and the consecration would have been completed." Suraqa then stood up and said, "Mohammed, is this dispensation temporary and intended for us, or is it permanent?" Mohammed said, "It is permanent." Meanwhile, Ali returned from Yemen and recited verses that corresponded to Mohammed's intent. (Another man said that Ali was reciting verses about Hajj that were similar to Mohammed's. Mohammed told Ali to continue to wear the consecration garments and to allow him to share the sacrifice.)

SEXUAL MUTILATION

M037,6676 A man was accused of fornicating with one of Mohammed's slave girls. Mohammed said to Ali, "Go and kill this man." Ali found the man cooling himself in a well, and said, "Come out." When the man emerged from the well, however, Ali noticed that the man had been castrated. Seeing this, Ali spared the man's life. Ali returned to Mohammed and explained, "The man does not have a penis."

This hadith refers to the circumcision of female genitalia. The Sunna of Mohammed is that he never forbade the removal of the clitoris, a common custom of his day.

M003,0684 An argument arose in Medina between a group of Helpers and Immigrants concerning bathing. The Helpers believed that bathing after sex was obligatory only if there is an ejaculation. The Immigrants believed that a bath is always obligatory after sex. Abu Musa said, "Let me settle the matter." He went to Aisha and asked and received her permission to speak. He said, "Aisha, beloved of the prophet, I want to question you about an embarrassing matter." Aisha said, "Do not be shy. Speak to me as you would your mother." Abu Musa then said, "When is a bath obligatory?" Aisha responded, "You have asked the right person. Mohammed has said that a bath is obligatory when a man is encompassed by a woman and their circumcised genitalia touch."

JIHAD AND SEXUAL CONDUCT

B6,60,139 While on jihad without our wives, many of us became sexually frustrated. We asked Mohammed, "Should we castrate ourselves?" Mohammed forbade that, but did allow us to take a woman as a temporary wife. He recited, "Oh believers! Do not forswear the good things that Allah has made legal for your enjoyment."

B7,62,130 Several of us became sexually frustrated while on jihad with no women. We asked Mohammed whether we should castrate ourselves. He forbade us from that action, but he did give us permission to take a temporary wife, which we could have simply by giving a woman a garment." Abdullah then recited the Koran:

> 5:87 *O, you who believe, do not forbid the good things that Allah allows you, but do not commit excess for Allah does not love those who commit excess.*

Rape of a Kafir female captive is jihad.

B7,62,137 Receiving female slaves as shares of spoils of war, we would practice coitus interruptus with them to avoid unwanted pregnancy. We asked Mohammed his opinion, and he asked us three times, "Do you really remove yourself?" He then said, "No soul that is not preordained to exist will be created."

LAWS ABOUT SEX

B3,48,817 Mohammed ordered an unmarried man exiled for a year and that he be lashed one hundred times for having illegal sexual intercourse.

B3,49,860 A Bedouin and another man went to Mohammed and the Bedouin said, "Settle our dispute using the laws of Allah." The other man said, "Yes, let Allah's law settle our dispute." The Bedouin said, "My son worked for this man and had illegal sex with his wife. Some said that my son must be stoned to death. To save my son, I gave a ransom of one hundred sheep and a slave girl. Islamic scholars, however, said that my son must be lashed one hundred times and be exiled for a year." Mohammed said, "According to Allah's law, your son must be lashed one hundred times and be exiled for a year. The sheep and the slave girl must be returned to you." Mohammed then said, "Unais, seize that man's wife and stone her until she is dead." Unais then went and stoned the woman to death.

MISCELLANEOUS

B7,72,774 Mohammed cursed effeminate men and masculine women. He said, "Throw such people from your homes." Mohammed ordered such a man to be turned out and Umar ordered such a woman turned out.

B4,54,460 Mohammed: "If a man asks his wife for sex and she refuses, causing him to go to sleep angry, the angels will curse her the entire night."

M008,3363 Jabir said that the Jews had an expression which said, "When a man has sex with his wife from behind, their child will have squinty eyes." Consequently, the verse was revealed,

> 2:223 Your women are your plowed fields: go into your fields when you like, but do some good deed beforehand and fear Allah. Keep in mind that you will meet Him. Give good news to the believers.

M008,3365 Mohammed: "It is all right if a man wants to enter his wife from behind or from on top, but he should enter the vagina."

M008,3371 Abu Sirma asked Abu Sa'id Al Khadri, "Have you heard Mohammed speak of *coitus interruptus?*" He answered that he had and he said, "We went to Bi'l-Mustaliq with Mohammed, and we captured some beautiful Arab women. Of course we wanted them sexually (our wives were not with us), but we also wanted a good ransom for them [pregnancy would lower their sale price]. As a sort of compromise, we decided that we would force sex with the women, but that we would practice *coitus interruptus*. We soon decided, however, to ask Mohammed. He said that it did not matter because every soul that is destined to be born, will be born."

A Kafir captive woman could be used for sex even if she was married and her husband was present.

M008,3432 Abu Sa'id Al-Khudri relates that while Mohammed was at the Battle of Hunain he sent a detachment to Autas and defeated the enemy there. Although Mohammed's soldiers captured many females, they were reluctant to force sex with them because their husbands were polytheists. Allah, however, then revealed to them that it was permissible as soon as a woman's menstrual cycle ended.

This is the Sunna of Mohammed

APOSTATES

CHAPTER 11

*33:21 You have an excellent example in Allah's Messenger
for those of you who put your hope in Allah and the
Last Day and who praise Allah continually.*

In Islam the option of killing an apostate, one who leaves Islam, is spelled out in the Koran, the Hadith, the Sira, and the early history of Islam after Mohammed's death.

When Mohammed died, entire tribes wanted to leave Islam. The first wars fought by Islam were against these apostates, and thousands were killed.

B2,23,483 After the death of Mohammed, Abu Bakr became the caliph, and he declared war against a group of Arabs who reverted back to paganism.

Umar asked Abu Bakr, "How can you war against these men when you remember that Mohammed said, 'I have been ordered by Allah to continue the fight until all the people say, "There is no god except Allah," and whoever says this will have his life and possessions protected from my anger. The exceptions being legal regulations that are adjudicated by man; Allah will settle all accounts.

Abu Bakr said, "I will fight those who argue that no difference exists between the tax [the poor tax was a Muslim obligation] and the prayer. The tax is an obligation put upon man by Allah. If someone should refuse to pay me even the smallest amount that they used to pay during the time of Mohammed, then I will fight them for doing so."

Umar then said, "Allah spoke to Abu Bakr, and I now know that he was right."

B9,83,17 Mohammed: "A Muslim who has admitted that there is no god but Allah and that I am His prophet may not be killed except for three reasons: as punishment for murder, for adultery, or for reverting back to non-belief after accepting Islam."

B9,84,57 Ali ordered that some atheists brought before him be burnt to death. Upon hearing this, Ibn Abbas said, "If it were me, I would not have ordered them burnt. Mohammed told us, 'Don't punish people with fire. That is Allah's punishment." I would have done as Mohammed instructed, 'Whoever turns his back on Islam, kill him.'"

Killing false Muslims is rewarded by Allah.

B9,84,64 If I [Ali] relate something to you that Mohammed said, I swear to Allah that I would rather be smashed to pieces than to put false words in his mouth. However, if I were to say something other than a Hadith to you, then it may very well be false because I may seek to trick my enemies.

Without question I heard Mohammed say, "In the final days there will be young fools who will say all the appropriate things, but their conviction won't go any further than their words, and they will flee their faith like an arrow flies from a bow. Wherever you find such people, kill them. Whoever kills them will be rewarded on Judgment day."

No punishment is too great for the apostate.

B8,82,797 Some people came to Medina and soon became ill, so Mohammed sent them to the place where the camels were sheltered and told them to drink camel urine and milk as a remedy. They followed his advice, but when they recovered, they killed the shepherd guarding the camels and stole the herd.

In the morning, Mohammed heard what the men had done and ordered their capture. Before noon, the men were captured and brought before Mohammed. He ordered that their hands and feet be cut off and their eyes gouged out with hot pokers. They were then thrown on jagged rocks, their pleas for water ignored and they died of thirst.

Abu said, "They were thieves and murderers who abandoned Islam and reverted to paganism, thus attacking Allah and Mohammed."

The verdict of Allah and Mohammed is to kill the Jewish apostate.

B9,84,58 Abu said, "I went to Mohammed and he said, 'Abu, go to Yemen.'"

Some time later Mohammed sent Muadh after Abu, and when he caught up to him, Abu placed a pillow on the ground and asked him to sit.

Muadh, seeing a bound man beside Abu asked, "Who is he?"

Abu answered, "He is a Jew who converted to Islam and then reverted."

Muadh said, "I won't sit down until you kill him. That is the thrice-repeated verdict of Allah and Mohammed for such people."

Abu then ordered the man slain. Abu then said, "We talked about that night's prayers and somebody said, 'I wish that Allah would reward me for sleeping as well as for praying.'"

Kill the apostate.

B9,89,271 A certain Jew accepted Islam, but then reverted to his original faith. Muadh saw the man with Abu Musa and said, "What has this man done?"

Abu Musa answered, "He accepted Islam, but then reverted to Judaism."

Muadh then said, "It is the verdict of Allah and Mohammed that he be put to death and I'm not going to sit down unless you kill him." [Death is the sentence for apostasy, leaving Islam.]

This is the Sunna of Mohammed

SATAN AND SUPERSTITIONS

CHAPTER 12

47:33 Believers! Obey Allah and the messenger,
and do not let your effort be in vain.

MAGIC

B4,53,400 Mohammed was hexed one time and mistakenly thought he had done things that he had not done.

A spell was put on Mohammed one time that caused him to believe he had done things that he had not done. He spent a long time praying to Allah and finally came to us and said, "Allah has shown me how break the spell."

I saw two people in a dream. One sat at my head and the other sat at my feet. The first man asked the other, "What is wrong with this man?" The second man said, "He is under a bewitching spell." The first man asked, "Who has cast the spell?" The second man answered, "Labid." "What did he use?" the first asked. The other man replied, "A comb with hair on it, and the pollen from a date palm." The first man then asked, "Where is it kept?" He was told, "In the Dharwan well."

Mohammed visited the well, and upon his return he told me that "the date palm trees near the well look like devil's heads." I asked if he had removed the charm that was used to bewitch him from the well, and he said that he had not. "No, Allah cured me. I don't want the people to be tempted to evil." Some time later the well was filled with earth.

EVIL EYE

B4,55,590 Mohammed would beseech Allah to protect Al-Hasan and Al-Husain. He would say, "Our ancestor, Abraham, would beseech Allah to protect Ishmael and Isaac by saying, "Allah, the Koran protects me from all venomous creatures and every evil eye.""

B7,71,636 Mohammed said, "There is no disputing the existence of an evil eye." He also forbade tattooing.

SATAN

M023,5044 Mohammed: "If someone drops food from his mouth, he should quickly pick it up, brush off any dirt, eat it, and never leave any for Satan. He should lick his fingers clean before wiping them with a towel, because no one knows what part of the food contains the blessing."

M023,5046 Mohammed: "Satan is with you in everything that you do. He is there when you are eating, therefore if you drop any food from your mouth, you should brush away any dirt and eat it. Do not leave any for Satan. When you finish eating, lick your fingers clean, because you do not know where the blessing resides in the food."

B2,21,243 Mohammed: "Satan puts three knots on the back of a sleeping persons head. On each knot he imprints these words, 'Stay asleep; the night is long.' When a person wakes up and thinks of Allah, one knot is untied; when a person performs purification, another knot is untied, when a person says his prayers, the third knot is untied and the person awakes with energy and a kind heart. If any knots remain, the person wakes up lazy with a vexing heart."

M024,5279 Mohammed: "The bell is Satan's musical instrument."

B2,22,301 One time after giving the daily prayer Mohammed said, "Satan faced me and attempted to disrupt my prayer, but Allah gave me strength and I strangled him. I considered tying him to a pillar in the mosque so that the people could see him in the morning. However, I recalled the words of Solomon, 'Lord, give me a kingdom the like of which will belong to no other.' Allah then forced Satan to return from where he came with his head bent low with shame."

B4,54,492 Someone mentioned to Mohammed a man that slept long after sunrise. Mohammed said, "Satan has urinated in that man's ears."

B4,54,500 Mohammed: "At dusk, keep your children near, because the devil is out. After an hour they may roam. Invoke Allah's name and close your house gates at night. Invoke Allah's name and cover your dishes. If your dishes lack covers, then place some wood or something over them."

B4,54,506 Mohammed: "When a person is born, Satan touches him with two fingers. Jesus, Mary's son, was the exception. Satan tried to touch him, but missed and touched placenta instead."

B4,54,509 Mohammed: "Satan causes yawning. If any of you yawn, stop as soon as you can. If you are yawning, before you know it, Satan will be causing you mischief."

B8,73,242 Mohammed: "Allah hates yawning and likes sneezing. The obligatory Muslim response to someone sneezing and giving praise to Allah is to say 'May Allah give you mercy.' Yawning, however, is caused by Satan. Stifle a yawn as soon as possible. If a person says, "Ha," while yawning, Satan will cause him mischief."

B4,56,714 I [Abdullah] was present when Mohammed pointed to the east and said, "Certainly, our troubles will begin here, where Satan's face emerges."

B7,69,527 Mohammed: "At dusk, keep your children inside, because that is when the devils roam. After an hour of night, however, they may go to their rooms and you may invoke Allah and close your doors. Satan can not open a shut door. Invoke Allah and cap your water bottle; invoke Allah and cover your dishes. Cover them however you may, and turn out your lights."

B7,71,643 I [Abu Qatada] was there when Mohammed said, "Allah gives good dreams, bad dreams are from Satan. If any of you experience something unpleasant during a dream, they should seek protection with Allah and blow three times to the left. This will protect you."

JINNS AND SPIRITS

Jinns are nonmaterial creatures who can help and hurt humans. Humans are made from earth and jinns are made from fire. Jinns occur in the Koran as well; one sura is titled "The Jinns."

B4,54,533 Mohammed: "Put lids on your pots and pans, cover your dishes, and put the cap on the water bottle at night. Lock your doors and keep a close eye on your children at night because that is when the jinns run amuck. Upon going to bed, put out the lights so that a rat can't cause a fire and burn the house down."

B5,58,199 Masruq and I [Abdur-Rahman] were talking and I asked him, "Who told Mohammed about the jinns listening to the Koran?" He replied, "Your father, Abdullah, told me that Mohammed heard about them from a tree."

B5,58,200 While accompanying Mohammed, I [Abu Huraira] spent some time carrying water for purification and cleaning. One time, Mohammed asked, "Who are you?" I answered, "Abu Huraira." He said, "Get me some stones so I may wipe my anus, and take care that you don't bring me any dried dung or bone."

I carried some stones over to him in the hem of my robe, left them by his side and I walked away. Later I asked him what was the significance of the bone and the dung and he said, "That is what jinns eat."

The jinn delegate from Nasibin—a very charming jinn—asked that they might have the residue from human food. I interceded with Allah for them that they might never be hungry as long as there was dung and bones for them to feed upon.

B1,8,450m Mohammed: "An enormous devil came and attempted to disrupt my prayers last night. Allah, however, gave me the strength to overcome him. I considered tying him to one of the mosque pillars so that everyone could see him as they came to pray, but I remembered what Solomon said:

> 38:35 He said, "Lord, forgive me and give me a kingdom that will be ruled by no other besides me, because you are truly the bountiful giver."

I released the demon and it slunk away, humiliated."

B1,12,740 Mohammed and several companions rode off, planning to go to the market. Simultaneously, a barrier sprang up separating the jinns from hearing the words from heaven and shooting stars began to rain down on them.

The jinns said, "The erection of this barrier is certainly a new occurrence. Some of you go East and some of you go West and see what has caused these strange circumstances. One group found Mohammed at Nakhla, near Tuhama. He and his companions were praying. When the jinns heard the Koran, they said, "I swear to Allah this is what prevents us from receiving word from heaven,"

The jinns returned home and told their people, "It is undeniable that we have heard a glorious Koran that clearly illuminates the true path. We are believers, and we will not acknowledge equals to Allah." The following verse detailing the conversion of the jinns was then revealed to Mohammed:

> 72:1 Say: It has been revealed to me that a group of jinn [the jinns are unseen beings created from fire] listened and said, "Truly, we have heard a wonderful recital. It guides us to the truth. We believe

in it, and we will never again worship another god. Exalted is the majesty of Our Lord! He has neither a wife nor a child. The foolish among us speak of a god that is unjust. We believed that no man or jinn would utter a lie against Allah."

This is the Sunna of Mohammed

MEDICINE, HEALTH, SCIENCE

CHAPTER 13

3:32 Say: Obey Allah and His messenger, but if they reject it,
then truly, Allah does not love those who reject the faith.

SCIENCE

B4,54,421One day as the sun was setting, Mohammed asked me [Abu Dhar], "Do you know where the sun goes at night?" I said, "You and Allah know better than I." Mohammed said, "It travels until it sits under the throne of Allah where it waits until permission is given to rise. A day will come when the sun will not be allowed to rest, nor continue on its regular path. It will instead be ordered to return the way it came and will rise in the west. That is how I interpret Allah's revelation:

> *36:37 The night is a sign for them. We withdraw it from the day and*
> *plunge them into darkness, and the sun runs its mandated course.*

B9,93,476 Mohammed: "There are five unseen keys known only to Allah: only Allah knows what will happen tomorrow; only Allah knows whether a child will be born as a male or a female; only Allah can predict the weather; only Allah knows when and where a person will die."

B8,74,246 Mohammed said, "Allah created Adam in the perfect human shape and size, nearly ninety feet tall. When Allah created Adam, he said, 'Go and introduce yourself to the angels sitting there. Pay attention to their greeting because that is the manner in which you and your descendents will greet others.' Adam went to the angels and said, 'As-Salamu Alaikum (Peace be upon you).' The angels responded, 'As Salamu-Alaika wa Rahmatullah (Peace and Allah's mercy be on you)."

Mohammed also said, "Everyone entering Paradise will do so in the perfect and original form and shape of Adam, rather than their present stature, which is continually diminishing."

B4,55,549 Mohammed said about human conception, for the first forty days after conception, each of us forms in a mother's womb. The next forty days is spent as a clot of blood, and the next forty as a bit of flesh. Then an angel is sent by Allah to write four determining words that signify a persons destiny: his actions, his time of death, his occupation, and whether he will be blessed or cursed by Allah. A soul is then infused in his body.

B4,55,546 Hearing of Mohammed's imminent arrival in Medina, Abdullah went to him and said, "I have three questions for you that only a prophet can answer: What is the first sign of the Hour of Reckoning? What will be the first meal served in Paradise? Why does a child look like his father, and why will it look like it's mother's brother?"

Mohammed said, "Gabriel has just given me those answers." Abdullah said, "Of all the angels, Gabriel is the greatest enemy of the Jews." Mohammed continued, "The first sign of the judgment is a great fire that unites the people of the east and the west; the people of Paradise will first dine on fish liver; if during intercourse the man climaxes first, the resulting child will look like him, if the woman climaxes first, then the child will look like her."

CURES

B4,54,483 In Mecca, I [Abu] often sat with Ibn Abbas. One time I had a fever and he told me, "Take Zam-zam water [a well in Mecca] to relieve a fever because Mohammed said a fever is caused by the heat from the fires of Hell; alleviate it with water, or Zam-zam water."

B7,67,446 Mohammed was asked about a mouse that fell into some butter fat and died. He said to dispose of the mouse and the butter-fat around it, but keep and eat the remaining butter fat."

B7,71,673 Mohammed: "If a fly drops into a container of liquid, submerge it in the liquid and throw the fly away. In one wing of the fly is a disease, but in the other is a cure for the disease."

B7,71,591 While traveling to Medina, Ghalib contracted an illness. Ibn Abi Atiq went to him and told us, "Treat the illness with black cumin. Grind five or seven seeds and add oil. Drop the mixture in both nostrils because Aisha related to me that she heard Mohammed say that black cumin can cure any disease except As-Sam. Aisha asked, 'What is As-Sam?' Mohammed replied, 'Death.'"

B7,71,592 I [Abu Huraira] was there when Mohammed said, "Black cumin can cure every disease except death."

B7,71,611 My son suffered from a disease of the throat and tonsils which I [Um Qais] had treated by pressing my fingers on his palate and tonsils. I took the boy with me to see Mohammed, and he asked me, "Why do press your son's throat and cause him pain? Treat him with Indian incense. It cures seven diseases, including pleurisy. To treat throat and tonsil disease, it is used as a snuff, and to treat pleurisy, it is placed in one side of the mouth."

Mohammed on disease.

B7,71,614 A man said to Mohammed, "My brother suffers from diarrhea." Mohammed said, "Tell him to drink honey." The man returned to Mohammed and said, "He drank the honey, but it made his condition worse." Mohammed said, "Allah tells the truth and your brother's stomach tells a lie."

This is the Sunna of Mohammed

BODILY FUNCTIONS

CHAPTER 14

58:20 *Those who oppose Allah and His Messenger will be laid low.*

Since Mohammed is the ideal pattern of Islam, and being a Muslim entails copying all his actions, the hadiths go into great detail about Mohammed's bodily functions. Here are a very few samples:

URINATION / DEFECATION

M002,0504 Salman testified that he was told: "You learn everything that you need to know from Mohammed, even about feces." Salman replied, "Yes. Mohammed has forbade us from facing the kiblah [Mecca] while defecating or urinating, or from wiping the anus with the right hand or wiping with fewer than three pebbles or with animal dung or a piece of bone."

B1,4,215 Mohammed was walking through a graveyard one time when he heard the voices of two people being tortured in death. At first, Mohammed said, "These people are being tortured for a great sin that we must take care to avoid." He quickly added, "Yes, they are being punished for a great sin. One never avoided soiling himself while urinating, and the other was a terrible gossip who instigated trouble among friends." Mohammed then asked for and received a leaf from a date-palm. He tore the leaf in two and put one half on each of the graves in question. When asked the significance of his act he said, "I hope that their punishment will be alleviated while these pieces of leaf dry."

B1,4,226 Abu Musa placed great importance on the manner of urination and was often heard to say, "If a Jew splashes urine on his clothes, he will cut away that piece of his garment." Having heard that, Hudhaifa commented to Abu Wail, "I wish that he didn't place such importance on urination." Hudhaifa continued, "Mohammed would urinate at garbage dumps while standing."

RITUALS OF ELIMINATION

B1,4,144 When Mohammed went to relieve himself, he would say, "Allah, protect me from evil spirits and from wicked actions."

B1,4,146 Mohammed: "If anyone must relieve themselves while in an open area, they should not face toward or away from Mecca. Instead, they should either turn to the west or the east."

B1,8,388 Mohammed said, "Do not face toward or away from Mecca while defecating. Instead face either west or east." Abu Aiyub also said, "Arriving in Sham, we found toilets facing Mecca. So, we used them, but turned our faces sideways and begged Allah to forgive us."

B1,4,147 It is commonly said, "While sitting and using the toilet, do not face Mecca." I [Abdullah] say to them, "One time, on the roof of my house, I saw Mohammed sitting on a couple of bricks while relieving himself. He was facing Jerusalem, but a screen shielded him."

B1,4,156 Mohammed: "Do not hold your penis or clean your genitals with your right hand. When drinking, do not breathe into the cup."

M003,0729 Upon entering a toilet, Mohammed would say: "Allah, protect me from that which is evil and foul smelling."

B1,4,157 One time I [Abu Huraira] followed Mohammed outside when he went to the bathroom. Without looking around, he said something like, "Get me some stones so that I may clean myself, and don't give me any dried dung or pieces of bone." I wrapped some stones in my robe and left them next to him and I went away. When he finished, he wiped himself with the stones.

B1,4,163 Mohammed: "When performing ablution, a person should place water in his nostrils and blow it out. Anyone that wipes his anus with stones should use an odd number of stones. Upon waking, a person should wash his hands before performing ablution because no one knows where his hands have been while sleeping."

FLATULENCE

B1,4,137 Mohammed: "A person at prayer who either urinates, defecates, or breaks wind must repeat ablution, or his prayer will not be accepted."

B1,4,139 Mohammed was asked by my uncle about an acquaintance who suspected that he may have broken wind while praying. Mohammed said, "Unless he either hears or smells something, he should not stop praying."

B1,8,436 Mohammed: "As long as a person is properly praying and does not break wind, the angels will continue to ask Allah's forgiveness for you. The angels say, 'Allah be merciful. Forgive him.'"

B8,73,68 Mohammed outlawed laughing at someone for breaking wind.

SPITTING

B1,8,404 Mohammed: "Nobody should spit directly in front of himself or to his right, rather he should spit to his left or beneath his foot."

This is the Sunna of Mohammed

ANIMALS

8:46 Obey Allah and His messenger, and do not argue with one another for fear that you will lose courage and strength.

DOGS

B1,4,173 Mohammed: "It is vital that a dish be washed seven times if a dog drinks from it."

B3,39,515 Mohammed: "One Qirat's worth of reward shall be deducted daily from a person's accumulated good deeds for owning a dog that doesn't hunt or guard a farm."

M024,5248 Noticing that Mohammed was quiet and grieving, Maimuna said to him, "Mohammed, you seem troubled today." Mohammed replied, "Gabriel promised that he would visit tonight, but he has not come." Now, Gabriel never broke a promise, so this strange behavior caused Mohammed to be depressed. Suddenly, however, Mohammed realized that a puppy had been sleeping under his bed. He ordered it to be removed from the house and he sprinkled water from his hand over the place where the dog had lain. Later that evening, when Gabriel visited, Mohammed said to him, "You promised that you would see me last night." Gabriel said, "I did promise, but an angel will not enter a house with a dog or a picture in it." Mohammed reacted to this revelation by ordering the death of all dogs, even the dog that was kept in the orchard. He did, however, exempt the dog that guarded the large fields.

B7,67,389 Mohammed: "Anyone who keeps a dog as merely a pet, and not a hunting or guard dog, shall have two Qirats deducted every day from his accumulated good deeds."

B4,54,540 Mohammed decreed that all dogs should be slain.

B1,9,490 I [Aisha] was told of several things that can negate a prayer. I was told, "Prayer is nullified by a dog, an ass, or a woman that passes before people in prayer." I said, "You have turned women into dogs."

M004,1032 Mohammed said, "If any of you stand for prayer with an object as big as a saddle's rear in front of you, or if an ass, a woman, or a black dog passes in front of you, your prayer will be blocked." Someone asked, "Abu Dhar, what is it about a black dog that makes it different from a red or a yellow dog?" Abu Dhar said, "I asked the same thing of Mohammed, and he said, "A black dog is a devil.""

M010,3813 Mohammed gave an order to kill dogs, which we obeyed so faithfully that we even killed the dog that accompanied a woman coming from the desert. Mohammed later rescinded this order, but he did say, "It is your obligation to kill a black dog even if it has white spots over the eyes because it is a devil."

B3,34,439 Mohammed banned receiving money in exchange for a dog, in exchange for sex, or in exchange for fortune telling.

SNAKES

B3,29,56 Several of us were in a cave with Mohammed when he recited a Sura that had just been revealed to him. When a snake suddenly appeared, Mohammed ordered us to kill it. We scrambled to slay the serpent, but it escaped. Mohammed said, "You have escaped the snake's evil, and it has escaped yours."

B4,54,518 I [Ibn Umar] witnessed Mohammed give a sermon. He said, "Kill snakes when you can. Take special care to kill any snake with two white lines down its back, or a snake with a stumpy or mutilated tail. They cause blindness and miscarriages."

B4,54,527 Mohammed: "Kill snakes with two white lines on their backs; they cause blindness and miscarriages."

B4,54,529 It was Ibn Umar's practice to kill snakes, but later he forbade the practice. He said, "One time Mohammed saw a snake skin that had been recently shed. He said, 'Find that snake and kill it.' It was because of this that I would kill snakes. I changed my practice when later Abu Lubaba told me that Mohammed had said, 'Do not kill all snakes, just those that have shortened or mutilated tails with two white lines down the back. Kill those snakes because they cause blindness and miscarriages.'"

OTHER ANIMALS

B4,55,579 Mohammed ordered that salamanders should be killed because, "They spit fire on Abraham."

B3,36,484 Mohammed banned the accepting of money for breeding fees.

B4,52,115 Mohammed allotted two shares of spoils of war to each horse and one share to each rider who participated in jihad.

B3,29,54 Mohammed: "It is not a sin for a pilgrim to slay certain animals: Crows, kites, mice, scorpions, and rabid dogs."

M020,4621 Mohammed: "Allah's blessings reside in the forelocks of war horses."

M035,6581 Mohammed: "If you hear a cock crowing, ask Allah for His good will because the cock sees angels. If you hear a donkey braying, ask Allah for His protection, because the donkey sees Satan."

This is the Sunna of Mohammed

ART

CHAPTER 16

*4:170 People! The Messenger has come to you with truth
from your Lord. If you believe, it will be better for you. But
if you do not believe, know that all that is in the heavens
and earth belongs to Allah. Allah is all-knowing and wise!*

B7,72,843 Mohammed grew depressed one day after Gabriel's promised visit was delayed. When Gabriel came at last, Mohammed complained about the delay. Gabriel said to him, "Angels will not enter a house that contains a dog or a picture."

B8,73,130 There was once a curtain with pictures of animals on it in my [Aisha's] house. When Mohammed saw it, his face became flushed with anger. He tore it to bits and said, "People that paint such pictures will receive Hell's most terrible punishment on Judgment Day."

B4,54,447 One time I [Aisha] created a stuffed pillow for Mohammed and decorated it with pictures of animals. He came in with some other people one day, and I noticed a look of excitement on his face. I asked, "What is wrong?" He replied, "What is that pillow doing here?" I answered, "I made that for you so that you could lie on it." He said, "Are you not aware that angels will not enter a house with pictures in it and that the person that makes such pictures will be punished on Judgment Day until he gives life to that which he has made?"

B3,34,428 Ibn Abbas and I were together one day when a man came to him and said, "Ibn Abbas, I am a painter and my livelihood comes from these pictures." Ibn Abbas said, "I only know what Mohammed tells me, and I heard him say, 'Anyone who paints a portrait will continue to receive Allah's punishment until he can bring the picture to life, which of course, a man can not do.'"

The man turned pale and he breathed a heavy sigh upon hearing this. Ibn Abbas said, "That is a shame. If you must make pictures, then my advice is to make pictures of inanimate objects, like trees."

This is the Sunna of Mohammed

MOHAMMED

CHAPTER 17

64:12 *So obey Allah and His messenger. But if you turn*
your backs to them, Our messenger is not to blame,
for his duty is only to deliver Our warning clearly.

HIS PHYSICAL APPEARANCE

B5,58,280 Pagans would part their hair, but Mohammed used to wear his hair falling loose like the people of the Scriptures. If not instructed differently, Mohammed would follow their example. Later, however, Mohammed began to wear his hair parted.

B7,72,787 Mohammed was neither tall nor short. His complexion was similarly muted, neither pale nor bronzed. His hair was not particularly curly or straight. He became Allah's Apostle at forty, spending thirteen years in Mecca and ten years at Medina. He died at the age of sixty.

B7,72,791 Qatada asked Anas to describe Mohammed's hair. Anas said, "Mohammed's hair reached almost to his shoulders. It was wavy. Not straight, but not very curly, either.

B7,72,793 Mohammed had a unique look to him. He had big feet and hands, but his palms were soft.

B4,56,751 Mohammed was of average height and had wide shoulders and long hair. I saw him wearing a red cloak one time, and I thought he was the most handsome man I had ever seen.

There are contradictory reports about the vanity of hair dyeing.

B1,4,167 Ubaid said to Abdullah, "I have seen you do some things that I have not seen anyone else do." Abdullah asked, "What things do you refer to?" Ubaid replied, "I have seen you wear tanned leather shoes. I have seen you dye your hair. Furthermore, you only touch the southern corners of the Kabah. Finally, when you are in Mecca the people do not perform the rituals in the same manner."

Abdullah responded, "First of all, I touch only the southern corners of the Kabah because that is what Mohammed always did. Next, I have certainly seen Mohammed wear tanned leather shoes; in fact, I have seen him perform the purification rituals wearing such footwear. Regarding the dyeing of my hair, I do it because I have seen Mohammed doing it."

B4,56,750 Qatada asked Anas, "Did Mohammed ever dye his hair?" Anas answered, "No, he only had a few gray hairs around his temples."

B7,72,783 Someone asked Anas if Mohammed dyed his hair. Anas told the person, "He did not have enough gray hair to dye. I could count the number of gray hairs in his beard."

B7,72,784 Uthman Bin Abdullah Bin Mauhab said, "I was sent to Um Salama with a small container of water with some of Mohammed's hair in it. It was an ointment that was used to treat the evil eye and other ailments. I looked in the container, and I could see some red hairs in it."

MOHAMMED'S WHITENESS

There are many hadiths that report Mohammed's whiteness.

B4,56,765 When Mohammed prostrated himself to pray, he would spread his arms so wide apart, that we could see his armpits. Ibn Bukair described it as "the whiteness of his armpits."

B9,90,342 At the battle of Al-Ahzab, Mohammed helped us carry dirt to the fortifications. We could see the dust covering his white belly.

B3,47,769 Mohammed delegated a man from the Al-Azd tribe to be a tax collector. When the man returned he said to Mohammed, "This is the money that I have collected for you and this money was given to me as a present."

Mohammed said, "If this man wanted presents, why didn't he stay at home with his parents? By Allah, if someone takes something from the tax collection, they will carry that weight around their neck on Judgment Day. If it is a camel, it will be grunting when he is judged; if it is a cow, it will be mooing; if it is a sheep it will be bleating." Mohammed then raised his hands up high, exposing his white armpits, and said, "Allah, haven't I told the people your instructions?"

B4,52,90 At the battle of Al-Ahzab I saw Mohammed carrying dirt which covered his white belly. He was saying, "Without your help Allah, we would have no guidance, we would neither pray nor give charitably. Give us peace and courage when we battle our enemies. Our enemies have rejected you and Mohammed, but we will never give up if they try to attack us."

B2,17,122 I [Abdullah Bin Dinar] once heard Ibn Umar recite some of Abu Talib's poetic verse: "And a white man (Mohammed) who is asked to pray for rain and who is the protector of orphans and the guardian of widows." Ibn Umar, Salim's father, relates the same story.

B1,3,63 We were sitting with Mohammed in the Mosque one day when a man rode up on a camel. He asked, "Which one of you is Mohammed?" We answered, "That white man leaning on his arm..."

B1,8,367 Just before the battle of Khaybar, we and Mohammed gave the Fajr prayer before sunup. I [Anas] was riding behind Abu Talha and next to Mohammed. We were so close, that as we rode down the main street of Khaybar, my knee touched Mohammed's leg. His garment moved and exposed the whiteness of his thigh.

B4,56,747 Rabia Bin Abi Abdur-Rahman heard Anas Bin Malik describe Mohammed like this: "For our people, he was average height. Not tall, but not short. He had an middling complexion, rosy, not pale white, but not dark brown either. His hair was wavy: not very curly, but not very straight. Allah first spoke to him when he was forty. He received Allah's revelations for ten years while in Mecca. He then stayed in Medina for another ten years. When he died, he had maybe twenty gray hairs on his head and in his beard." Rabia said, "One time I saw some of his hair and it was red. I was told that perfume had turned it red."

HIS ANGER

There are many hadiths about Mohammed's anger.

B1,2,19 If Mohammed ordered a Muslim to do something, he made sure that it was something that was easily done, something within their limits of strength or endurance. Still, many complained, "Mohammed, we can't do that. We are not like you. Allah has freed you from all sin." The anger was apparent on Mohammed's face and he said, "No one fears Allah more than I, and I know Allah better than any of you."

B1,3,90 A man once said to Mohammed, "I may not be able to go to the obligatory prayer because our Imam is very long-winded when he leads the ceremony." The narrator continued, "I had never seen Mohammed more angry. He said, 'Some of you are making the others dislike praying. If you lead the prayers, then you should keep it brief. Some of the people are sick, weak, or simply have work to do.'"

HIS CURSES

B9,85,73 Mohammed would beseech Allah in this prayer, "Allah, Save the weak Muslims. Be cruel to the Mudar and smite them with years of famine and hunger just as you brought famine to the people during the time of Joseph."

HIS WIFE AISHA

Aisha was his favorite wife. This dream occurred when she was six.

M031,5977 Aisha quotes Mohammed: "Three nights in a row I saw you in a dream. An angel delivered you wrapped in silks and said, 'This is your wife.' As I unwrapped the silk, your face appeared. I said, 'If this dream is indeed from Allah, then let Him make it happen.'"

B5,58,234 I [Aisha] became engaged to Mohammed when I was six years old. We then moved to Medina where I became ill and my hair fell out. My hair grew back and one day my mother, Um Ruman, came to fetch me while I was playing with some girl friends. I had no idea what she wanted, but she grabbed me by the hand and told me to stand by the door. I was out of breath, but when my heart stopped racing, she scrubbed my face and head with water.

We then went into the house where several Helper women were waiting. They said, "Good luck. May Allah bless you. Best wishes." My mother then handed me over to the women who began to prepare me. Shortly and quite unexpectedly, Mohammed came and I was handed over to him. I was nine years old at the time.

M008,3309 Mohammed and I [Aisha] were married when I was six. I was brought to his house when I was nine. We moved to Medina where I fell sick with a fever for a month. My hair fell out as a result of the illness. My mother, Um Ruman, came for me one day as I was playing on a swing with some friends. I had no idea what she wanted, but she took me by the hand and had me stand by the door of our house. I was out of breath, but when I had composed myself, my mother took me inside and handed me over to some of the Helper women who proceeded to wish me good luck. The women washed me and made me pretty. Mohammed came in the morning and I was given to him.

B7,62,65 Mohammed and Aisha were married when she was six. They consummated the marriage when she was nine. Hisham said, "I was told that Aisha stayed with Mohammed from the age of nine until his death."

B8,73,151 My girl friends and I [Aisha] would play with dolls while in Mohammed's presence. They would try to hide when he entered, but he always would call them back to play with me. Playing with dolls or anything with a human image was forbidden, but because I was so young, not yet having reached puberty, it was allowed.

M031,5981 Aisha relates that she and her friends often played with dolls while Mohammed was present, but when he came over, her friends would hide from him because of shyness. He would, however, call them back to play with her.

M008,3312 Mohammed made our marriage contract during Shawwal and took me into his house during Shawwal. I [Aisha] was his favorite wife, and I desired that all the women of my family become brides during Shawwal."

M008,3451 I [Aisha] never found a woman who showed me more affection than Sauda, a wife of Mohammed. I wish that I was as compassionate as she. When she grew old, 40, she gave over to me the day allotted to her to spend with Mohammed. She said to Mohammed, "I have given over to Aisha the day that I spend with you." Consequently, Mohammed gave Aisha two days, her regularly scheduled day and Sauda's day.

HIS OTHER WIVES

B3,47,755 The wives of Mohammed collected themselves in two groups. The first group consisted of Aisha, Hafsa, Safiya, and Sauda. The other group was made up of Um Salama and his other wives. The Muslims all knew that Mohammed loved Aisha, so if someone had a gift to give Mohammed, they would wait until he was staying at her home.

This made the wives in Um Salama's group jealous and they sent Um Salama to the prophet to request that he tell the people to send their gifts to him in whoever's house he happened to be in. Um Salama made the request to Mohammed several times, each time getting no reply. Finally, he answered her by saying, "Do not try to hurt me on Aisha's account. Allah's revelations do not come to me when I am not in her bed." Um Salama said to him, "I apologize to Allah for causing you pain."

The wives remained unhappy, so they sent Mohammed's daughter, Fatima, to him. Fatima said to Mohammed, "Your wives ask that you treat them as well as you do Abu Bakr's daughter, Aisha." Mohammed said to her, "Do you love what I love?" She said that she did, and when the jealous wives asked her to intercede with her father again, she refused.

Finally, they sent Zainab to him. Zainab was bitter and spoke harshly as she asked that Aisha be shown no favoritism. Zainab began to shout and scold and abuse Aisha to her face. Aisha then vigorously answered Zainab's complaints until she was left silent. Mohammed looked at Aisha and said, "She is certainly Abu Bakr's daughter."

B3,47,766 Mohammed would draw lots to determine who would accompany him on his journeys. Each wife would be given a day and night, and he would take whoever's name was selected. Sauda, however gave up her turn to Aisha because she knew that would please Mohammed.

B7,62,22 While traveling from Khaybar to Medina, Mohammed stopped for three days to celebrate and consummate his marriage to Safiya. The wedding banquet offered no meat or bread, but Mohammed ordered leather sheets to be spread and dates, butter, and dried yogurt were laid out upon it.

The people wondered if Safiya was going to be Mohammed's slave-girl or his wife. Someone said, "If she is ordered to veil herself, then she will be his wife. If she is not compelled to veil herself, she will be his slave girl." When Mohammed proceeded to Medina, Safiya rode behind Mohammed on his camel, shielded from the sight of the people with a screening veil.

This is a story about Mohammed's family life. He had been given a beautiful Coptic pleasure slave. He set the slave up in a separate apartment away from the mosque and the other wives. The wives became angry because he spent so much time with her and she became pregnant with a male child. None of Mohammed's wives in Medina ever got pregnant.

B7,62,119 Umar and I [Ibn Abbas] were performing our Hajj obligation when Umar had to stop to urinate. I came along carrying a vessel of water so that he might wash his hands and perform ablution afterwards. I had been curious about something, so I took the opportunity to ask, "Umar, who was Allah referring to when he revealed the verse:

> 66:4 *"If you both [Hafsa and Aisha] turn in repentance to Allah, your hearts are already inclined to this, but if you conspire against the Messenger, then know that Allah is his protector, and Gabriel, and every just man among the faithful, and the angels are his helpers besides. Perhaps, if he [Mohammed] divorced you all, Allah would give him better wives than you—Muslims, believers, submissive, devout, penitent, obedient, observant of fasting, widows, and virgins."*

Umar said, "I'm shocked that you ask, Ibn Abbas. The verse refers to Aisha and Hafsa."

Umar recited the hadith and elaborated further, "A neighbor of mine, who was a Helper, and I would take turns visiting Mohammed to inform him of important news. He would go one day, and I the next.

"Well, our tribe, the Quraysh, used to keep our women under our control in Mecca, but when we moved to Medina, our women began to copy the Helper women who bullied their men. One day I shouted at my wife and she began to talk back to me in a very disagreeable manner. She said, 'Why does it surprise you to hear me talk back to you? Mohammed's wives talk back to him. Some of them even refuse to talk to him for an entire day.'" The conversation frightened me and I said, 'Whoever did that will surely be punished.' I left the house and went to see my daughter, Hafsa, one of Mohammed's wives. I asked her, 'Do you, or any of Mohammed's wives bicker at him so much that he remains angry all day?' She said, 'Yes.' I said, 'You are a foolish woman. Are you not concerned that Allah will become angry with you for angering Mohammed? You will be ruined. Stop bickering with your husband. Quit talking back to him, and certainly do not ignore him by not speaking to him. If you need something, ask me. Don't copy Aisha. She may be able to get away with such behavior, but she has more charm than you do and besides, Mohammed likes her better than you."

"I continued, 'There was a rumor that the Ghassan tribe were readying their cavalry to invade our territory. So one day, my companion, the Helper, returned from town and visiting Mohammed when he came to my house and banged violently on the door. I was very alarmed and so I went outside to see him. He said, 'Something big happened today.' I asked, 'Have the Ghassan invaded?' He replied, 'No, something even bigger and more terrifying. Mohammed has divorced his wives.'"

"Umar said, 'So Mohammed has separated from his wives. Hafsa is ruined.' I had been half expecting him to divorce Hafsa, but the news shocked me nevertheless. After dressing, I went to pray with Mohammed, who immediately afterwards secluded himself in an upstairs room. I went to Hafsa and found her weeping. I asked her, 'Why are you crying? Didn't I warn you about your behavior? Has he divorced all of his wives, or just you?' She replied, 'I don't know. He has kept himself alone in the upstairs room.'"

"I left her quarters and joined a group of people sitting near the pulpit. They were weeping and clearly upset. I sat awhile but couldn't take it. I went to the room where Mohammed was staying and asked his black slave, 'Will you ask Mohammed's permission for Umar to see him?' The slave went in for a moment, but quickly came out and said, 'I told Mohammed, but he would give no answer.'"

"I left and again sat with the people around the pulpit but soon became depressed. I returned to Mohammed's room and again said to his black slave, 'Umar would like permission to speak with Mohammed.' He returned after a moment and said, 'I told him you were here, but he would not answer.'"

"I rejoined the people near the pulpit, but quickly couldn't bear the tension, so I went to the slave for a third time and said, 'Will you ask permission for Umar to speak with Mohammed?' He went in and soon returned saying, 'I told him you wished to speak, but he refused to answer. I began to leave when the slave called me back and said, 'Mohammed has given you permission to speak.'"

"I entered the room and saw Mohammed lying on a bed made from the stalks of date palm leaves. There were no sheets or blankets on the bed to protect the skin and Mohammed's skin was marked by the date palm stalks. He was leaning on a leather pillow when I greeted him. I said, 'Mohammed, have you divorced your wives?'"

"He said, 'No.'"

"I replied, Allah is great.' I stood there a moment, and asked Mohammed, 'Can I tell you something? The Quraysh [Mohammed and Umar were members of this Meccan tribe] used to be able to control their women, but when we emigrated to Medina, we discovered that their women had power over the men.' Mohammed just smiled. So I said to him, 'May I tell you something else? I spoke to Hafsa and told her, "Do not act like Aisha, because you are not as charming as she is and Mohammed loves her more.'"

When I saw Mohammed smile at this, I sat down and looked at the poor furnishings in the room. The only things of value in the room were three leather hides. I said, 'Mohammed, ask Allah to make your people wealthy. The Romans and the Persians are rich, and their people enjoy the earthly pleasures, even though they reject Allah.'"

"Mohammed quickly sat up and asked me, 'Do you mean to tell me, son of Al-Khattab, that the Romans and Persians are rewarded for their good and virtuous behavior?'"

"I said, 'Oh, of course not. Beg Allah to forgive me.'"

"Mohammed remained separated from his wives for twenty-nine days. His anger being precipitated by a story about himself and a slave-girl that Hafsa told Aisha. Because of his anger toward them, Mohammed had sworn, 'I will not rejoin my wives for an entire month.'

It was about this time that Allah scolded his prophet for setting aside his wives."

When twenty-nine days had passed, Mohammed went to Aisha, who asked him, 'Husband, you had sworn to remove yourself from our company for a month, but only twenty-nine days have passed. I know because I have been counting the days.'

"Mohammed told her, 'This month has twenty-nine days.'"

"Aisha later said, 'That was when Allah revealed the verse concerning the divorce option. From all of his wives, he chose me first, and I, in turn, chose him.' He then gave the same option to his other wives and they all wished to remain his wife.'"

SEX

B1,5,248 Mohammed would bathe after sex by first washing his hands and performing ablution just as he would for praying. He would then dip his fingers in water and rub his scalp. Then he would drizzle three handfuls of water over his head and pour the rest over his body.

B1,5,249 Narrated by Maimuna, a wife of Mohammed: After sex, Mohammed purified himself just as he would for prayer except that he would not wash his feet. He would rinse off the semen and vaginal secretions from his penis and then pour water over the rest of his body. He would then remove his feet from the bathtub and wash them. That was how Mohammed cleaned himself after sex.

B1,5,258 After taking the bath of *janaba* [sexual relations or wet dreams] Mohammed would perfume himself. He would take the scented solution in his hand and first rub it on the right side of his head, then the left side, and finally down the middle of his head using both hands.

B7,71,660 Magic was used upon Mohammed that caused him to think that he had sex with his wives, when in fact he had not. One day he said to Aisha, "I have had a revelation from Allah about that problem that has been bothering me. Two men came to me in a dream; one of them sat by my head and the other at my feet. The first one asked the other, 'What is this man's problem?' The other replied, 'He is under a magic spell.' The first man asked, 'Who's spell is he under?' The other man answered, 'Labid, a hypocrite and an ally of the Jews.' The first man then asked the other, 'What was used to cast the spell?' 'A comb with Mohammed's hair in it,' he was told. 'Where is this comb?' the first man asked. 'In a bag made from a date palm. It is hidden under a rock in the Dharwan well,' the other man told him."

Mohammed went to Dharwan and removed the bag containing the comb. He said, "That was the well I saw in my dream. Its water was the color of Henna and the date palms surrounding it resembled the heads of devils. I took out the bag with the hexed comb in it." Aisha said to Mohammed, "Why didn't you take Nashra to treat your malady?" Mohammed said, "It was not necessary. Allah had already cured me. Besides, I don't want evil (magic) to establish itself among the people."

LITERACY

The frequent claim about Mohammed is that he was illiterate, making the Koran all the more a miracle. However, Mohammed was a businessman for twenty years before he became a prophet. It is hard to imagine that he could not do arithmetic or read invoices and business contracts.

This hadith implies writing skills.

B1,3,114 When Mohammed was on his deathbed, he said "Bring me something to write with and some paper. I will write you instructions that will keep you on the right path after I am gone." Umar, however, complained, "Mohammed is very sick. Besides, we have the Koran and that is enough to keep us from going astray."

A heated argument broke out among the companions about whether or not to obey Mohammed's request. Angered at the commotion, Mohammed said, "Get out of here and leave me alone. You do wrong by bickering in front of me." Ibn Abbas left the room and said, "It is disastrous that the argument prevented Mohammed from writing those instructions."

VISIT TO PARADISE

This is one of the best known stories about Mohammed.

B1,8,345 Mohammed: "When I lived in Mecca, I had a dream that my roof opened up and the angel Gabriel descended from Paradise. He opened my chest and cleansed it with Zam-zam [a sacred well in Mecca] water. He then filled my chest with wisdom and faith from a golden tray, before closing me up."

"He took me by the hand and we rose toward the nearest heaven. Gabriel said to the first gatekeeper, 'Open the gates.' The gatekeeper asked, 'Who are you?' The Angel replied, 'It is Gabriel.' The gatekeeper asked, 'Do you have anyone with you?' Gabriel replied, 'Yes, Mohammed is with me.' The gatekeeper asked, 'Has he been summoned?' Gabriel said, 'Yes.' The gates were opened for us and we entered the nearest heaven where we saw a man sitting with people on his right and left side. The man laughed when he looked to the people on his right, but he cried when he looked at the people on his left. The man then said to me, 'Welcome, holy Prophet and holy son.' I questioned Gabriel, 'Who is that man?' Gabriel answered, 'That is Adam and the people around him are the souls of his descendents. The people on his right are in Paradise and those on his left are in Hell.'"

"We ascended from the first heaven to the sixth heaven. After meeting Adam, we met Idris, Moses, Jesus, and Abraham. (Anas relates: "Abu Dhar said that Mohammed met Adam, Idris, Moses, Jesus, and Abraham but does not mention in which particular heaven they resided, although he does say that Adam was on the nearest heaven and Abraham was on the sixth heaven. When Gabriel and Mohammed passed Idris, he said to Mohammed, 'Welcome, holy prophet and holy brother.' Mohammed asked Gabriel, 'Who is that man?' Gabriel said, 'That is Idris.'")"

Mohammed continued, "We passed Moses, who said, 'Welcome, holy prophet and holy brother.' I questioned who that man was and Gabriel said, 'That is Moses.' We then passed Jesus who said, 'Welcome, holy prophet and holy brother.' Again I asked, 'Who is that man?' Gabriel replied, 'That is Jesus.'"

"We then passed Abraham who said, 'Welcome, holy Prophet and holy brother.' I asked Gabriel, 'Who is that man?' Gabriel said, 'That is Abraham.' Gabriel and I then ascended to the seventh heaven where I heard pens creaking. There Allah gave me fifty prayers which he ordered my followers to recite. As I passed Moses, he asked, 'What has Allah ordered your followers to perform?' I answered, 'He has given them fifty prayers to recite.' Moses said, 'Return to Allah and ask that the number be reduced, because your people can not bear so many.' I returned to Allah and asked that the number be reduced and he cut the number in half. As I passed Moses again, I told him that the number was reduced by half and he said, 'Go to Allah again and ask that the number be further reduced, because your people will not be able to bear the load.' I returned to Allah and he assented to again lower the number by half. As I passed Moses again, we spoke and he said that the number was still too much for my people to bear. I went to Allah again and this time he said, 'Here are five prayers. Each of them is rewarded equal to fifty, because my message doesn't change.'"

"Once again Moses and I spoke as I passed him, and once again he urged me to return to Allah and ask that the number be reduced. I said, however, that I was reluctant to beseech Allah another time. Gabriel instead took me to the furthest border of heaven. It was wrapped in indescribable colors.

There I was admitted into Paradise, where walls were made of pearl and the land was entirely of musk."

There is conflict in the hadiths about whether Mohammed performed miracles. The Koran agrees with this hadith that he did not. However, there are hundreds of hadiths that relate his miracles. The Sira is filled with supernatural knowledge of the future and of what happened in far places.

B6,61,504 Mohammed: "The other prophets were given the power to perform miracles in order to convince the people, but I was given the Divine Inspiration of Allah's revelations. My hope is that on Judgment Day, my followers will outnumber the other prophet's followers."

HABITS

B1,4,169 Mohammed would perform all tasks by working from right to left. This included putting on his shoes, combing his hair, or washing himself.

B1,6,298 Mohammed and I [Aisha] would bathe together after sex in the same tub. During my period, he would have me wear a dress that only covered me from the waist down and he would fondle me. He would also let me wash his head while I was menstruating.

B2,15,73 Mohammed would always eat dates before going to prayer on the Day of 'Id-ul-Fitr. Anas also related: "Mohammed would eat a lot of dates."

B4,54,428 Aisha said that Mohammed would become very agitated if he saw a cloud in the sky. He would pace back and forth, continually enter and exit his house and his face would change color. If it rained, however, he would become relaxed. Aisha always recognized that mood of his. When she asked about it he said, "I don't know why I'm afraid. It might be the same agitation that the people of Ad referred to in the Koran:

> 46:24 *Then they saw a cloud coming into their valley. They said, "The cloud is bringing us rain." No, it is the scourge you sought, a wind that carries agonizing retribution. Everything was destroyed by the command of the Lord. Morning rose on empty houses—the reward of the guilty.*

B9,92,458 Mohammed said, "Anybody who eats onions or garlic should keep their distance. They should stay away from the Mosque and stay at home." Ibn Wahb said, "One time in Badr, some cooked vegetables were brought to Mohammed. He caught an aroma that disagreed with him and he said, "Bring that here." When Mohammed identified the food as some that he disliked, he said to his companion, "Eat this. I can't because I often have to whisper to people that you don't speak with."

B7,65,292 Mohammed preferred to begin things from the right side; combing his hair, putting on his shoes, or performing ablution. He would follow this practice in every thing he did.

M023,5018 Anas said that Mohammed forbade people to drink while standing. Qatada related: We asked him, "What about eating while standing?" Anas said, "That is even more objectionable."

M023,5029 Anas related the story that Mohammed would drink his refreshments in three gulps.

M023,5037 Mohammed: "When a Muslim eats, they should not wipe their hand until it is licked clean, either by themselves or by someone else."

M024,5175 Mohammed saw me [Abdullah B. Amr] wearing some clothes dyed in saffron one time and he asked, "Did your mother make you wear those clothes?" I said, "I'll wash them." He said, "No, burn them."

M024,5231 Mohammed: "When someone puts on sandals, he should put the right one on first. When someone takes off sandals, he should take off the left one first. Either this or simply put them on or take them off at the same time."

M024,5234 Mohammed made it illegal for a man to eat with his left hand or walk with only one sandal on. He also forbade a man to wear a garment that had no opening for the arms to extend or support himself when wearing a single garment that might expose his genitalia.

M024,5238 Mohammed: "No one should lie on his back with one foot placed on top of the other."

MODESTY

Mohammed seems to have been exceptionally modest about his body.
B1,8,360 One day Mohammed and other Meccans were hauling stones to be used in construction at the Kabah. His uncle, Al-Abbas saw him toiling in his izar (waist cover) and said to him, "You should take off your izar and drape it over your shoulder to protect the skin from the rough stones." Mohammed did so, but soon passed out. Since that time, he was never seen in the nude.

B7,72,807 One day a man peeped into Mohammed's house and saw him scratching his head with a comb. Noticing the man Mohammed said, "If

I had realized that you were peeking at me I would have stuck this comb in your eye. The reason that people must ask permission is to keep them from seeing things that they shouldn't."

MOHAMMED'S SLAVES

The woman that Mohammed's "right hand possessed" was a captive used as a slave for his pleasure in sex.

B9,89,321 Mohammed would only take a pledge of allegiance from a woman if she first recited this Koranic verse:

60:12 O, Messenger, when believing women come to you and pledge an oath of allegiance to you and ascribe no other gods as partners to Allah ...

Mohammed would never allow his hand to touch a woman's hand unless she was a woman that his right hand possessed, that is his slave or one of his wives slaves.

Another example of how slaves were common in Mohammed's life.

B2,22,325 I [Kuraib] was ordered by Ibn Abbas, Al-Miswar, and Abdur-Rahman to speak to Aisha on their behalf and to question her about her reciting two Rakat prayers after giving the Asr prayer. They instructed me to say, "We were told that you say those prayers, even though we are informed that Mohammed has forbade the people from saying them." Ibn Abbas added, "Umar and I used to thrash people when we caught them saying those prayers." I relayed their message to Aisha and she said, "Speak to Um Salama about those prayers." I returned to Ibn Abbas, Al-Miswar, and Abdur-Rahman and told them what Aisha said and they replied, "Repeat our question to Um Salama." Um Salama answered, "I remember Mohammed banning the recital of those two prayers after the Asr prayer, but later I saw him give them right after giving the Asr prayer."

Some time later Mohammed came to my house while I was sitting with some female Helpers from the Bani Haram. I ordered my slave-girl to stand next to Mohammed and repeat Um Salama's words to him, "I saw the prophet forbid the saying of the Rakat prayers after the Asr prayer but then saw him give those very same prayers." I told the girl, if he beckons to you, wait until he finishes praying, then listen carefully to his words." The girl did as I instructed and when the prophet had finished his prayer, he called the slave-girl over to him and said, "You ask about the pair of Rakat prayers being said after the Asr prayer. I had become distracted by the people's business and did not have the time to give the two Rakat prayers after the Zuhr prayer. The two Rakat prayers you speak of were the two that I had missed earlier."

B3,34,351 A man committed himself to freeing one of his slaves upon his death, but later needed money. Mohammed took the slave and asked, "Does anyone want to buy this slave from me?" Nu Aim received the slave from Mohammed after giving the Prophet a certain price.

B3,46,717 I, Ibn Aun, wrote Nafi a letter, and his reply said that the forces of Mohammed had initiated a surprise attack on the Bani Mustaliq when they were watering their cattle and not paying attention. Their men were slain and their women and children were seized. A woman, Juwairiya, was given to Mohammed as spoils of war that day. Nafi's letter said that he had heard the account from Ibn Umar, who was in the attacking army that day.

B3,47,765 Narrated by Kurib, a freed slave of Ibn Abbas: "Maimuna, one of the Prophet's wives, told me one day that she had freed one of her slave girls without first asking Mohammed's permission. When it was her turn to stay with Mohammed, she said, 'Are you aware that I have freed my slave girl?' He replied, 'Really?' 'Yes,' she said. Mohammed said, 'Your reward would have been greater if you had given her to one of your mother's brothers.'"

B7,65,344 While at the house of his slave tailor, Mohammed ate a gourd dish that he seemed to enjoy. Ever since then, I [Anas] have enjoyed eating gourd.

B7,64,274 Upon hearing that Mohammed had recently received some new slave girls, his daughter, Fatima, went to him to complain that working a stone hand mill hurt her hand.

She could not find her father immediately, so she shared her complaint with Aisha. Aisha relayed this complaint to Mohammed. Ali, Fatima's husband, tells us, "We had already gone to bed one night when Mohammed arrived. We wanted to get up and greet him, but he said, "Don't get up." He sat between Fatima and myself and I could feel his cold feet pressing against my belly. He said, "May I show you something better than what you ask for? Before going to bed say 'Subhan Allah' thirty-three times, 'Alhamdulillah' thirty-three times, and 'Allahu Akbar' thirty-four times; this will be worth more to you than another slave girl."

B8,78,698 We fought alongside Mohammed at the battle of Khaybar, and although we did not receive any gold or silver as spoils of war, we did get miscellaneous property like clothes. However, a tribesman of the Bani Ad-Dubaib, Rifaa Bin Zaid, gave Mohammed a slave named MidAm.

In the Al-Qura valley, MidAm was killed by an arrow shot by an unknown person. Some people said, "Congratulations to MidAm for getting to Paradise." Mohammed cried, "No, MidAm is not going to Paradise. By Allah, the sheet that he stole from the Khaybar spoils of war is burning over him in Hell." When the people heard what Mohammed had to say, one man returned a couple of leather straps that he had taken from the spoils of war. Mohammed said to him, "One strap of fire or two straps of fire for you."

B9,91,368 Umar sought Mohammed and found him in an upstairs room with a black slave standing guard at the top of the stairs. Umar said to the slave, "Inform Mohammed that Umar is here and seeks permission to see him." The slave then admitted me to the room.

M010,3901 A slave came to Mohammed and pledged to migrate to Medina. Mohammed did not know the man was a slave until his master came and demanded that he be returned. Mohammed said, "Sell the slave to me." Mohammed gave the man two slaves in exchange for the one who pledged migration, but later would not accept a pledge from anyone without first determining whether he was free.

WAR

Mohammed was devoted to violence in the cause of Islam.

B9,90,332 Abu Huraira overheard Mohammed say, "By Allah, if I had a way of transporting all the men who wished to fight in jihad, I would not miss any opportunity to fight the Kafir. It would be a pleasure to be martyred for Allah, be resurrected, and martyred again and again."

B4,52,151 Mohammed and Abu Talha would share a shield in battle. Abu Talha was an exceptional archer, and Mohammed would follow the flight of his arrows as they sped toward their target.

Humor in jihad.

M031,5932 Amir B. Sa'd reported, on the authority of his father, that Allah's Apostle gathered his parents for him on the Day of Uhud when a polytheist had set fire to (i.e. attacked fiercely) the Muslims. Thereupon Allah's Apostle said to him: "(Sa'd), shoot an arrow, (Sa'd), may my mother and father be taken as ransom for you." I drew an arrow and I shot a featherless arrow at the Meccan polytheist, aiming his side. He fell down and his private parts were exposed. Allah's Messenger laughed so that I saw his front teeth.

RACISM AND MOHAMMED'S TRIBE

A member of Mohammed's Arab tribe is to rule over all Muslims.

B4,56,700 Mohammed said, "The Quraysh have first right to rule over the Muslims. People have different natures. Muslims follow the best Muslims. Kafirs obey the best Kafirs. The best and most qualified people in the days before Islam are the best people in Islam, if they fully understand the religious doctrine. You will discover that the best rulers are those who hate authority, that is, until they receive pledges of allegiance.

CRUELTY

B2,24,577 Some people came to Medina, but the climate made them sick, so Mohammed gave them permission to stay among the camels that had been collected for taxes. He told them to drink the camel's urine and milk, as that would cure their illness. However, the people instead murdered the shepherd and stole the camels. Mohammed sent men after them and they were quickly captured. Mohammed ordered that their hands and feet be cut off, and their eyes pierced with hot pokers. They were left to die of thirst on the rocks of Harra.

HIS BODILY FUNCTIONS

One of many hadiths about Mohammed and elimination.

B1,9,479 Whenever Mohammed went to the toilet, another boy and I would follow with a stick, a staff and a container of water. When he finished, we would give him the water.

NUMBER OF YEARS IN MECCA AND MEDINA

B5,58,190 Mohammed received his first revelation when he was forty. He remained in Mecca for thirteen years before being told by Allah to migrate. He stayed in Medina for ten years before passing away.

This is the Sunna of Mohammed

THE KORAN

CHAPTER 18

> 4:136 *Believers! Believe in Allah and His Messenger*
> *and in the Scriptures which were sent down to His*
> *Messenger and in the Scriptures He sent down before him.*
> *Those who deny Allah, His angels, His Scriptures, His*
> *messengers, and the Last Day have gone far astray.*

Islam holds that the Koran is complete, universal, perfect, and contains the exact words of Allah. It contains no mistakes, no omissions or errors. The Koran existed before creation. Some of its history is contained the hadiths.

The story of Mohammed's first revelation.

B1,1,3 Mohammed's revelations began a series of good dreams that surpassingly came true, and which were followed by strong inclination for solitude. He would seclude himself in a cave at Hira, worshiping Allah for days on end until longing for his family drove him home. He would take large quantities of food, enough to last through his retreat and take him home again to his wife, Khadija. On a retreat just like this, Mohammed's revelations descended suddenly upon him.

An angel materialized before him and asked him to read. Mohammed said, "I can not read." The angel grabbed him and squeezed so hard he almost fainted. The angel again asked him to read. Again Mohammed said, "I can not read." The angel said nothing, but grabbed Mohammed so tightly, that he thought that his bones would break. After a time the angel again asked Mohammed to read, but for a third time Mohammed said, "I can not read." The angel grabbed Mohammed and said,

> 96:1 *Recite: In the name of your Lord, Who created man from*
> *clots of blood.*
> 96:3 *Recite: Your Lord is the most generous, Who taught the use*
> *of the pen, and taught man what he did not know.*

As quickly as he could, Mohammed returned home, his heart pounding and the effects of his revelation consuming him. He ran to his wife, Khadija, and said, "Hide me! Hide me!" She covered him with robes and blankets until he was composed and was able to describe what happened to him. He said to her, "I am afraid that something is going to happen to me." Khadija replied, "Nothing is going to happen to you. Allah will protect you. You have good relationships with your family and friends, you give to charities, you are generous to your guests, and you always help those in trouble."

Khadija took Mohammed to see her cousin, Waraqa, who had converted to Christianity before the advent of Islam. Waraqa was a scribe, quite skilled in writing with the Hebrew alphabet, even though he was old and blind. Speaking to Waraqa, Khadija said, "Cousin, listen to what your cousin Mohammed has to say." Mohammed told Waraqa what had occurred. Waraqa thought for a moment and said, "The angel that appeared to you was Gabriel, the same angel that Allah sent to Moses. I can only wish that I will still be alive and young when your people drive you away." Waraqa said, "Yes. All prophets have been met with distrust and hostility. I will fight to defend you if I am alive when you are expelled, but I am old." Within a few days, Waraqa died and Mohammed's revelations ceased for a time."

Mohammed later said, "I was walking when suddenly, a voice from above spoke to me. Looking up, I saw Gabriel sitting on a chair, suspended between the earth and sky. He frightened me, so I ran home and said to Khadija, "Cover me with blankets." Allah then revealed to me these verses:

> 74:1 *You [Mohammed], wrapped up in your robe, get up and sound the alarm.*
> 74:3 *Magnify your Lord. Purify your garment. Run from abomination. Do not give favors with the thought of reward. Wait patiently for your Lord. When the trumpet sounds, it will be a terrible day, a day without rest for the Kafir.*

Mohammed's revelations then came regularly, frequently, and with great strength.

Many verses in the Koran were replaced by later ones. Some of the verses contradict each other.

B6,60,60 I [Ibn Az-Zubair] told Uthman, "Why do you include this verse in the Koran? It has been abrogated (replaced) by another verse.

> 2:240 *If you should die and leave behind a wife, you should leave her at least enough to live a year in the home; but if she leaves on her own, you are not to blame for her lawful actions."*

Uthman replied, "Let it remain nephew because I will not move anything in the Koran from its original location."

B6,60,70 Mohammed recited this verse:

3:7 *It is He who has revealed the Scriptures to you. Some of its verses are clear and basic in their meaning. These are the foundation of the Book, and others are metaphorical. Those whose hearts have a tendency to err follow the metaphorical verses seeking to cause arguments when they attempt to interpret them. Only Allah knows their meaning. And those who are firmly grounded in knowledge say, "We believe in it. All of it comes from our Lord," but only those who possess understanding will listen*

Mohammed then said, "If you see those who follow what is not entirely clear, then they are deviates from the truth. Beware of them."

B6,61,507 As caliph, Uthman directed Zaid, Said, Abdullah, and Abdur-Rahman to collect and collate the Koran. He said to them, "If any of you do not agree with Zaid about his use of the Arabic in the Koran, then they should compose the verse in the language of the Quraysh because the Koran was also revealed in that dialect." They heard and obeyed.

The production of the first Koran as a book:
B6,61,509 After a number of Mohammed's companions were killed at the Battle of Yamama, Abu Bakr called me [Zaid Bin Thabit] to him for an audience. I found him sitting with Umar. Abu Bakr said, " Umar has said to me that a great number of those who have memorized the Koran were killed at Yamama. He is afraid that parts of the Koran will be lost as more of our pious soldiers are killed in battle, or simply die. He suggested to me that the Koran be collected and written down." I asked Umar, "Can you do that which Mohammed did not do?" Umar responded, "It is a good project and it needs to be done. He kept pressuring me until finally Allah opened my heart to the idea."

Abu Bakr then said to me, "You are wise and young. We have no doubts about your faith, and you formerly wrote Mohammed's revelations for him. Therefore, we feel that you should collect the fragments of the Koran and collate them into one volume."

I felt that moving a mountain would be easier than collecting the verses of the Koran. I asked Abu Bakr, "How can we do something that Mohammed did not do?"

Abu Bakr answered, "It is a good project and it needs to be done." Abu Bakr kept pressing me to accept the project until Allah opened my heart to the idea as he had Abu Bakr's and Umar's.

I began collecting the Koranic verses from bits of bone, stone, parchment, date palm leaves, and also from the memories of those who had memorized it until I had discovered the last Verse of Repentance:

> 9:128 *Now a Messenger has come to you from among yourselves. He is full of concern for you that you will fall into distress. He is compassionate and merciful to the faithful. If they turn away say, "Allah is sufficient for me. There is no god but Allah, and in Him I put my trust. He is the Lord of the glorious throne."*

I gave the completed manuscript of the Koran to Abu Bakr. He kept it until his death, when it was given to Umar. Umar had it until his death when it was given to his daughter, Hafsa.

Uthman, the caliph, burned all of the original source documents that went into preparing what we call the Koran today.

B6,61,510 During the war between the people of Iraq and Sham, Hudhaifa went to Uthman and informed him that he was concerned about the differing manners of reciting the Koran. Hudhaifa said to Uthman, "Caliph, save our people before they begin to fight over the Koran like the Jews and the Christians fought over their scriptures."

Uthman directed Hafsa to send him the manuscripts of the Koran so that perfect copies might be compiled. Uthman then directed Zaid, Said, Abdullah, and Abdur Rahman to make perfect copies. He told the men from the Quraysh, that if they disagreed with Zaid's translation, then they should write copies in the language of the Quraysh because the Koran was also revealed in that dialect.

The men did as they were told, and they made many copies. Uthman returned the original to Hafsa and sent a copy to every Muslim district. Once this was done he ordered all previous copies, fragments, or materials to be destroyed.

Said said, "I missed one verse that I recalled Mohammed reciting. We found it in Khuzaima's possession."

> 33:23 *Some among the believers have been faithful in their covenant with Allah. Some of them have fulfilled their covenant with their deaths, and some are waiting for death, and they have not wavered in their determination.*

B6,61,513 Mohammed: "The Koran was recited to me by Gabriel in one manner. I asked him to read it in another fashion, and then in another. Eventually he read it to me in seven different dialects."

B6,61,515 I [Yusuf] was with Aisha, Mohammed's beloved and the mother of all Muslims, when an Iraqi came to her and asked, "What is the best type of shroud?" Aisha said, "Allah have mercy on you. Why is that important?" He replied, "Let me see your copy of the Koran." Aisha asked him why and he said, "So that I may arrange a copy. People are reciting copies that are not in the correct order."

Aisha replied, "Why is the order important? You just need to know that the first sura to be revealed came from Al-Mufassal, and it talked about Paradise and Hell. After the people began to accept Islam, the verses speaking of the differences between the legal and the illegal was revealed. If the first verse to be revealed was the one regarding drinking alcohol, then people would say, "We can not give up alcohol." If the first verse to be revealed spoke of illegal sexual contact, the people would say, "We can not give up fornication."

I was a little girl in Mecca when this verse was revealed to Mohammed:

54:46 No! The Hour of Judgment is their promised time, and that hour will be terrible and bitter.

I was with him when the "Cow" and the "Woman" suras were revealed to him. Aisha then took her copy of the Koran and recited the Koran to the man in the correct order.

B6,61,524 By Allah! There is no chapter of the Koran but what I [Ali] know where it was revealed. There is no verse in the Koran that I don't know who it is about.

Mohammed's memory was the sole source of the Koran.

B6,61,562 One night in the mosque as Mohammed listened to a man reciting the Koran, he exclaimed, "May Allah bless that man. He has reminded me of verses and chapters that I had forgotten."

B1,1,2 Al-Harith asked Mohammed to describe how the Koran was revealed to him. Mohammed said, "At times it came like a bell ringing. This is the most difficult part of Divine Inspiration, and it lasts until I understand the revelation. Other times an angel visits me in the body of a man and his speech and meaning are clear to me." Aisha added, "It is true that I saw Mohammed have a revelation on a cold day and the sweat ran down his face as the episode ended."

Originally, there were seven versions of the Koran.

B3,41,601 Hisham recited one chapter of the Koran differently from my [Umar's] manner. Mohammed had taught me to read it the way he read it, so after prayers, I grabbed him physically and dragged him to

Mohammed and said, "He is not reciting the Koran in the manner you taught me."

I released Hisham and Mohammed asked him to recite the chapter in question. Afterward, Mohammed said, "That is the way it was revealed." Then he asked me to recite the chapter, and again, Mohammed said, "That is the way it was revealed. The Koran was revealed seven times, in seven styles. Recite it the way that is easiest for you."

B4,54,442 Mohammed: "After hearing Gabriel recite the Koran, I continually asked him to read it to me in differing ways. Eventually he read it to me in seven different dialects."

This is the Sunna of Mohammed

SHARIA LAW

CHAPTER 19

*4:59 Believers! Obey Allah and obey His Messenger
and those among you with authority. If you have a
disagreement about anything, refer it to Allah and His
Messenger if you believe in Allah and the Last Day.
This is the best and fairest way to settle a dispute.*

Islam is a complete political, cultural, legal, and religious system. Muslims believe the system came directly from Allah, so it is perfect and eternal. The political goal of Islam is for every constitution and every form of government to be replaced by the sacred form of government, the Sharia. All governments of the Kafirs are offensive to Allah. They are man-made and, therefore, not divine. It is historically inevitable that they will be replaced by the Sharia; it is simply a matter of time since it is the will of Allah.

The Sharia is the practical conclusion of political Islam. It is also a way for the Kafir to see how the Trilogy forms the basis of not only for a religion but also for the most powerful political system in history. The Trilogy is both a political theory and a complete, detailed code of law that covers contract law, banking, family law, insurance, criminal law, and foreign policy.

The following is from a thirteen-hundred-year-old classic text, *The Reliance of the Traveller.*[1] Due to the fact that the Koran is considered to be unchangingly perfect and final, it is still used today. Once you have read the Koran and the Hadith, you will recognize all of these laws. They are nothing more than a codified summary of both texts. The Sharia is the fruit of the doctrine of political Islam.

JIHAD

Jihad is war against Kafirs. The scriptural basis for jihad, prior to scholarly consensus, is such Koranic verses as:

*2:216 You are commanded to fight although you dislike it. You
may hate something that is good for you, and love something that
is bad for you. Allah knows and you do not.*

---

1.   Ahmad Ibn Naqib Al-Misri, *The Reliance of the Traveller, A Classic Manual of Islamic Sacred Law* (Amana Publications, 1994).

143

4:89.... *But if they turn back, find them and kill them wherever they are.*
9:36... *Do not be unjust to yourselves regarding them, but fight the Kafirs as they fight you altogether.*

and hadiths:

B2,23,483 *"I have been commanded to fight people until they testify that there is no god but Allah and that Mohammed is the Messenger of Allah, and perform the prayer, and pay zakat. If they say it, they have saved their blood and possessions from me, except for the rights of Islam over them. And their final reckoning is with Allah";*

M041,7015 *"To go forth in the morning or evening to fight in the path of Allah is better than the whole world and everything in it."*

The details of jihad are found in the Sira. Mohammed personally led twenty-seven expeditions; he fought in eight of them, killing only one person at the battle of Uhud. He sent others out on forty-seven expeditions. [This was over a period of nine years, or the average of one violent event every six weeks.]

THE OBLIGATORY CHARACTER OF JIHAD

Jihad is a communal obligation. The Prophet's saying,

"He who provides the equipment for a soldier in jihad has himself performed jihad,"

4:95 *Believers who stay at home in safety, other than those who are disabled, are not equal to those who fight with their wealth and their lives for Allah's cause [jihad]. Allah has ranked those who fight earnestly with their wealth and lives above those who stay at home. Allah has promised good things to all, but those who fight for Him will receive a far greater reward than those who have not.*

Jihad is personally obligatory upon all those present in the battle lines and to flee is a great wrong. Only if a soldier is ill, wounded, or without a weapon may he leave a battle. He may also leave if the opposing Kafir army is more than twice the size of the Muslim force.

Jihad is also obligatory for everyone when Kafir forces enter Muslim lands. The Kafirs must be repelled by every possible means.

Every able-bodied man who has reached puberty and is sane is called upon to serve in jihad.

THE OBJECTIVES OF JIHAD

Before declaring war upon Jews, Christians, and Zoroastrians they must first invite them to submit to Islam, and if they will not, then invite them to be dhimmis and pay the poll tax (jizya).

> 9:29 *Make war on those who have received the Scriptures [Jews and Christians] but do not believe in Allah or in the Last Day. They do not forbid what Allah and His Messenger have forbidden. The Christians and Jews do not follow the religion of truth until they submit and pay the poll tax [jizya], and they are humiliated.*

FLEEING FROM COMBAT IN JIHAD

Allah Most High says,

> 8:16 *Anyone who turns his back on them, unless it is for a tactical advantage or to join another company, will incur Allah's wrath and Hell will be his home, truly a tortuous end*

THE RULES OF WARFARE

It is not permissible in jihad to kill women or children unless they are fighting against the Muslims. It is permissible to kill old men and monks.

Whoever submits to Islam before being captured may not be killed or his property confiscated, or his young children taken captive.

When a child or a woman is taken captive, they become slaves and the woman's previous marriage is immediately annulled.

It is permissible in jihad to destroy their property and assets.

TRUCES

In Sacred Law, *truce* means a peace treaty with those hostile to Islam, involving a cessation of fighting for a specified period, whether for payment or something else.

There must be an advantage in making a truce other than mere preservation of the status quo. Allah Most High says,

> 47:35 *Therefore, do not be weak and offer the Kafirs peace when you have the upper hand for Allah is with you and will not begrudge you the reward of your deeds.*

Interests that justify making a truce are such things as Muslim weakness due to of lack of numbers or materiel, or the hope an enemy will become Muslim. If the Muslims are weak, a truce may be made for ten years if necessary, for the Prophet made a truce with the Quraysh for that long. A truce may not last longer than ten years.

THE SPOILS OF BATTLE

A free male Muslim who has reached puberty and is sane is entitled to the spoils of battle when he has participated in a battle until the end of it.

After personal spoils of war, the collective spoils of the battle are divided into five parts. The first fifth is set aside for Islam, and the remaining four-fifths are distributed to the fighters. A token payment may be given at the leader's discretion to women, children, and Kafir participants on the Muslim side.

A combatant only takes possession of his share of the spoils at the official division.

A fighter may carry off as much war booty from the battle as he can personally take away.

KAFIR SUBJECTS OF THE ISLAMIC STATE, THE DHIMMI

A *dhimma* is a formal agreement of protection is made with Jews and Christians. Such an agreement may not be effected with those who are idol worshippers, or those who do not have a Sacred Book or something that could have been a Book.

Such an agreement is only valid when the subject peoples follow the rules of Islam and the rules involving public behavior and dress. Only in their private lives are the subject communities to have their own laws, judges, and courts, enforcing the rules of their own religion among themselves pay the Kafir poll tax (*jizya*)

THE DHIMMI POLL TAX

Kafir subjects are obliged to comply with Islamic rules about the safety and indemnity of life, reputation, and property. In addition, they are penalized for committing adultery or theft, though not for drunkenness and are distinguished from Muslims in dress. They must always defer to a Muslim in public. The dhimmi may not build higher than or as high as the Muslims' buildings. They are forbidden to openly display wine or pork, to ring church bells or display crosses, recite the Torah or Gospels aloud, or make public display of their funerals and feast days and are forbidden to build new churches.

They are forbidden to reside in the Hijaz, meaning the area and towns around Mecca, Medina, and Yamama, for more than three days.

A Kafir may not enter the Meccan Sacred Precinct (Haram) under any circumstances, or enter any other mosque without permission.

If Kafir subjects of the Islamic state refuse to conform to the rules of Islam or to pay the dhimmi poll tax, then their agreement with the state has been violated.

A dhimmi may not commit adultery with a Muslim woman or marry her. Dhimmis may not conceal spies of hostile forces, nor lead a Muslim away from Islam. They cannot kill a Muslim nor mention something impermissible about Allah, the Prophet, or Islam

APOSTATES

Leaving Islam is the worst sin. When a sane person voluntarily leaves Islam, he should be killed.

There is no penalty for killing an apostate, since it is killing someone who deserves to die.

If a spouse in a consummated marriage leaves Islam, the couple are separated for a waiting period consisting of three intervals between menstruations. If the spouse does not submit to Islam the marriage is annulled.

THE PENALTY FOR FORNICATION OR SODOMY

The legal penalty is obligatorily imposed upon anyone who fornicates or commits sodomy.

An offender is not scourged in intense heat or bitter cold, or when he is ill and recovery is expected (until he recovers), or in a mosque, or when the offender is a woman who is pregnant, until she gives birth and has recovered from childbed pains. The whip used should be neither new nor old and worn-out, but something in between. The offender is not stretched out when scourged, or bound as his hands are left loose to fend off blows, or undressed, and the scourger does not lay the stripes on hard (by raising his arm, such that he draws blood). The scourger distributes the blows over various parts of the body, avoiding the vital points and the face. A man is scourged standing; a woman, sitting and covered.

If the penalty is stoning, the offender is stoned even in severe heat or cold, and even if he has an illness from which he is expected to recover. A pregnant woman is not stoned until she gives birth and the child can suffice with the milk of another.

In more than one place in the Koran, Allah recounts how he destroyed homosexuals. It is even more vile and ugly than adultery.

Allah Most High says:

26:165 *What? Of all the creatures of the world, will you have sexual relations with men? Will you ignore your wives whom Allah has created for you? You people exceed all limits!"*

The Prophet said:
Kill the one who sodomizes and the one who lets it be done to him. May Allah curse him who does what Lot's people did. Lesbianism by women is adultery between them.

MASCULINE WOMEN AND EFFEMINATE MEN

The Prophet said men are already destroyed when they obey women. The Prophet cursed effeminate men and masculine women. The Prophet cursed men who wear women's clothing and women who wear men's.

THE WIFE'S MARITAL OBLIGATIONS

4:34 *Allah has made men superior to women because men spend their wealth to support them. Therefore, virtuous women are obedient, and they are to guard their unseen parts as Allah has guarded them. As for women whom you fear will rebel, admonish them first, and then send them to a separate bed, and then beat them. But if they are obedient after that, then do nothing further; surely Allah is exalted and great!*

2:223 *Your women are your plowed fields: go into your fields when you like, but do some good deed beforehand and fear Allah. Keep in mind that you will meet Him. Give good news to the believers.*

It is obligatory for a woman to let her husband have sex with her immediately when he asks her; at home; and she can physically endure it. If sex will harm her she does not have to comply.

THE HUSBAND'S RIGHTS

A man has all rights to his wife's body. He is entitled to take her with him when he travels.

PERMITTING ONE'S WIFE TO LEAVE THE HOUSE

A husband may permit his wife to leave the house for religion and to see her female friends, or to go to any place in the town. A woman may not leave the city without her husband or a member of her unmarriageable kin accompanying her. All other travel is unlawful.

The husband may forbid his wife to leave the home because the Prophet said,

"It is not permissible for a woman who believes in Allah and the Last Day to allow someone into her husband's house if he is opposed, or to go out if he is averse".

DEALING WITH A REBELLIOUS WIFE

Examples of rebelliousness are when a wife gives a cold answer or does not submit to sex when he asks. He should not hit her but tell her, "Fear Allah concerning the rights you owe to me."

He can explain that rebelliousness means that he does not need to support her or it could be to inform her, "Your obeying me is a religious obligation."

If she commits rebelliousness, he may hit her but not in a way that injures her, meaning he may not bruise her, break bones, wound her, or cause blood to flow. It is unlawful to strike another's face. He may hit her whether she is rebellious only once or whether more than once.

It is permissible for him to hit her if he believes that hitting her will bring her back to the right path, though if he does not think so, it is not permissible. *His hitting her may not be in a way that injures her,* and is his last recourse to save the family.

THE CONDITIONS THAT ENTITLE A WIFE TO SUPPORT

The husband is only obliged to support his wife when she does not refuse him sex at any time of the night or day. She is not entitled to support from her husband when she does not obey him, even if for a moment or travels without his permission.

INJURIES

There is no obligatory indemnity for killing a Kafir at war with Muslims, someone who has left Islam, someone sentenced to death by stoning for adultery (by virtue of having been convicted in court), or those it is obligatory to kill by military action.

> 4:92 *A believer should never kill a Muslim unless an accident occurs. Whoever kills a fellow Muslim by accident must free one of his believing slaves and pay blood-money to the victim's family unless they give it to charity. If the victim was a believer from a people at war with you, then freeing a believing slave is enough. But if the victim was from a people with whom you have an alliance, then his family should be paid blood-money and a believing slave must be set free. For those who cannot afford to do this, they must fast for two months straight. This is the penance commanded by Allah. Allah is all-knowing and wise!*

4:93 *For those who intentionally kill another Muslim, Hell will be their punishment, where they will live forever.*

JUDGMENT, HELL, AND PARADISE

4:14 *But those who disobey Allah and His Messenger and go beyond His limits, will be led into the Fire to live forever, and it will be a humiliating torment!*

These are some religious hadiths about Judgment Day, Hell, and Paradise.

JUDGMENT

Predestination is a frequent theme of the Koran.

B2,23,444 Several of us were following a funeral procession. Mohammed joined us and we all sat together, with him in the center. He sat with his head bent and he scratched at the earth with a small stick. He said, "Every one of you, and every soul ever created has an assigned place either in Paradise or in Hell. Every soul has a predetermined fate, whether it be blessed or damned." One man asked, "Shouldn't we rely on the Koran to guide us? Surely the blessed among us will perform the actions of a blessed person and the damned among us will perform the actions of a damned person?" Mohammed said, "Good deeds are easy for the blessed person, just as bad deeds are easy for the person who is damned."

> 92:5 *He who gives alms and fears Allah and accepts the good, to him We will make the path to happiness easy. But he who is greedy and does not think he needs Allah's help and calls the good a lie, to him We will make the path to misery easy. And what good will his wealth do him when he dies?*

B2,23,456 Mohammed: "When a Muslim dies two angels will come to him and ask, 'In life, what did you say about Mohammed?'

"The faithful Muslim will testify, 'I said that he was Allah's slave and his prophet.' The angels will say to him, 'Look, that is your place in Hell. Because of your faith, Allah has given you a place in Paradise instead.' Thus he sees both possible destinations of his soul.

"A Kafir, or a hypocrite, however, will answer the same question by saying, 'I did not know the man,' or 'I said what the other people said.' The angels will say to such a person, 'You neither knew the man nor did you take his guidance by reading the Koran." Such a person will then be struck by a great hammer, causing him to cry out loudly enough for all except jinns and humans to hear."

B3,43,620 Mohammed: "When Muslims safely cross over the bridge spanning Hell, they will be detained at another bridge separating Hell and Paradise. There they will retaliate against each other for the transgression committed during life. This will purify them from sin and they will then be admitted into Paradise. Their place in Paradise will be more familiar to them than their home in the mortal realm."

The form of worship determines your eternal destiny.

B6,60,105 People asked Mohammed, "Will we see Allah on Judgment day?" Mohammed replied, "Of course. Do you have trouble seeing the Sun at noon on a cloudless day?" "No," the people answered. Mohammed asked, "Do you have trouble seeing the full moon on a cloudless night?" "No," the people answered. Mohammed said, "Just as you have no trouble seeing the Sun and Moon, you will have no trouble seeing Allah on Judgment day."

On Judgment day, an announcement will come, "Let all people follow the object of their worship." Everyone that did not worship Allah will go to Hell. The only people remaining will be Muslims and some Jews and Christians. The Jews will be asked, "Who did you worship?" They will reply, "We worshiped Ezra, the son of Allah." They will be told, "You lie. Allah has no wife or son. What do you want?" The Jews will say, "We want something to drink, we are thirsty." They will be collected in a Hell-fire that appears as a mirage, and they will be asked, "Will you drink?" They will then descend into Hell.

Next the Christians will be asked, "Who did you worship?" They will reply, "We worshiped Jesus, the son of Allah." They will be told, "You are liars. Allah has no wife or son." They will fall into Hell just as the Jews did.

Then only Muslims will remain, regardless of whether they were obedient or not. Allah will then appear to them in the form that each expects. They will be asked, "What are you waiting for? Each person will follow that which they worshiped in life." They said, "We are waiting for Allah." Allah will say, "I am your lord." And the people will reply, two or three times, "We only worship Allah."

B6,60,149 While delivering a sermon, Mohammed said, "Muslims, you will be brought before Allah naked, shoeless, and uncircumcised," He then quoted the Koran:

21:04 *Just as We made the first creation, so We will reproduce it. This is a promise We are bound to. Truly it is something We will fulfill.*

Continuing, Mohammed said, "Abraham will be the first human dressed on Judgment day. Indeed, some of my followers will be brought forward, only to be pushed into Hell, and I will say, "Allah, but they are my companions." Allah will respond, "You are unaware of their actions after you left them." I will reply as Jesus did:

5:117 *"I only said what You commanded me to say, 'Worship Allah, my Lord and your Lord,' and I was a witness of their actions while I was among them. When You caused me to die, You watched them, and You are witness of all things.*

Allah will then reply, "Since you left them, these people became apostates."

Mohammed is spiritually superior to Adam, Noah, Abraham, Moses, and Jesus. Islam holds that Mohammed is the most ideal man in all of history and all of creation.

B6,60,236 As Mohammed was eating some cooked meat that was prepared just as he liked it, he said:

"On Judgment day, I will be the leader of all the people. Do you know why? Allah will gather on one great plain every person who was ever born. They will be gathered together to hear the announcer's voice and to be viewed by the watcher. The sun will be so close, the people will suffer unbearable distress and pain."

"The people will say, 'Can we not find someone to intercede for us?' Some will cry out, 'Go to Adam.' They will say to him, 'You are the father of mankind. Allah made you with his own hands and breathed his spirit into you. He ordered the Angels to bow down before you. Intercede with him and stop our suffering.' Adam will say, 'Allah is angrier today than ever before, and he will never be this angry again. I was forbidden to eat the fruit, but I disobeyed. I need someone to intervene for me. Me! Me! Me!'"

"The people will cry out, 'Seek another. Go to Noah.' The people will say to Noah, 'Please intercede for us. We suffer greatly. You are the first of Allah's messengers. Allah has called you a grateful slave. Help us.' Noah will say, 'Allah's anger is greater today than it ever was or ever will be. I had the opportunity to make an invocation guaranteed to be granted, and I made it against my own people. Me! Me! Me!'"

"The people will cry out, 'Seek another. Go to Abraham.' The people will say to Abraham, 'Abraham you are Allah's messenger. Intercede with

Allah to stop our suffering. Abraham will say, Allah has become angrier today than ever before, and he will never be this angry again. I told three lies. Me! Me! Me! Seek another. Go to Moses.'"

"The people will go to Moses and say 'You are Allah's messenger and greater than the previous prophets because Allah has spoken directly to you. Intercede for us and beg Allah to stop our suffering.' Moses will reply, 'Allah's anger is greater today than it ever was or ever will be. I killed a man without his authorization. Me! Me! Me! Seek another. Go to Jesus.'"

"The people will go to Jesus and say, 'You are Allah's messenger and his message that he sent through Mary. Allah created your superior soul, and you spread his word while still a child. Please intercede with Allah for our sake. Can you not see how we suffer?' Jesus will respond, 'Allah's anger is greater today than it ever was or ever will be.' Jesus will not mention any specific sin, but will say, 'Me! Me! Me!'"

"The people will cry out, 'Go to someone else. Go to Mohammed.' So the people will flock to me and say, 'Mohammed, you are Allah's messenger and the last prophet. Allah has forgiven all your sins. Intercede with Allah. Can you not see our anguish?' I will say, 'I will stand before the throne of Allah and bow down before him. Allah will instruct me how to praise and glorify him and assuage his anger. Allah will instruct me as he has no other. Allah will say to me, 'Mohammed, lift up your head. Ask and your wish will be granted. Intercede and your pleas for your followers will be granted.' I will lift up my head and say, 'Mercy for my followers, Allah. Mercy for my followers.' Allah will then say, 'Mohammed, direct those followers of yours without accounts to settle to enter Paradise from the gate on the right. The other gates will be shared among the rest of the people.'"

Mohammed added "By Allah, the distance between the gates of Paradise is comparable to the distance between Mecca and Rome."

B7,71,606 Mohammed said, "I had a vision of Judgment day. The nations of the world were grouped together and displayed before me. A prophet or two would walk by with a few followers. A prophet would walk by with no followers. A large group of people walked by, and I asked, 'Are those my followers?' I was told, 'No, that is Moses and his followers. Someone said, 'Look at the vast group that fills the horizon. Those are your followers. Seventy thousand of them shall enter Paradise without being judged.'"

Mohammed then entered his home, opting not to tell his followers who made up the group of seventy thousand. The people began to clamor amongst themselves, wondering who would be in the group of seventy thousand Muslims that would enter Paradise without being judged beforehand. The people said, "We are the people that believe in Allah and have followed Mohammed; those people must either be ourselves, or our children that will be born in the Islamic era because we were born in the era of ignorance before Islam."

When Mohammed heard the commotion, he came outside and said, "The people you refer to are those who do not practice magic, they do not believe in good or bad omens, they do not practice ritual scarification, and they put their trust only in Allah." Upon hearing that, Ukasha asked, "Mohammed, am I one of those you refer to?" Mohammed said, "Yes." Another person asked, "Am I one of those you refer to?" Mohammed said, "Ukasha asked first."

B8,76,535 Several of us were in a tent with Mohammed and he asked, "Would you be happy to be one-fourth of the people in Paradise?" We replied, "Yes." He asked, "Would you be happy to be one-third of the people in Paradise?" We answered, "Yes." He then asked, "Would you be happy to be one-half of the people in Paradise?" We responded, "Yes." Mohammed then said, "I wish that you will make up half the people in Paradise because no one but a Muslim will enter Paradise, and you stand out when compared with other Muslims like a white hair on a black ox."

B8,76,555 Mohammed: "Standing at the gate of Paradise, I noticed that most of the people who had entered were poor, while the wealthy were required to wait outside while their accounts were settled. Meanwhile, the people condemned to Hell were being driven into the fire. As I stood there watching, I noticed that most of these people were women."

B9,93,481 Mohammed: "People will be tossed into Hell, and Hell will keep saying, 'Are there more?' until Allah places his foot over the entrance causing its sides to contract and it cries out, 'Enough.' Paradise will have space available for more people until Allah makes more people who will be allowed to live in the unused spaces of Paradise."

B9,93,541 Mohammed: "Paradise and Hell argued before Allah. Paradise asked, 'Allah, what wrong have I committed that only the poor and meek enter my gates?' Hell said, 'It is my fortune to be filled with the boastful and vain.' Allah placated them and told Paradise, 'You are Mercy,' and said to Hell, 'You are Retribution, which I use to punish whomever I choose. You will both be filled by my command.' Mohammed continued, 'Regarding Paradise, it will contain the virtuous because Allah will not harm the good creatures that he has created. Allah created Hell to punish whomever he chooses. Those people will be forced into its fires until it asks three times, 'Are there more?' Finally Allah will place his foot over the mouth of Hell until it is filled, its sides closing in on one another and it says, 'No more, no more, no more.'"

B4,54,416 Mohammed: "After Allah created the heavens and the earth, He declared that 'My Mercy overwhelms My Anger.'"

HELL

A jihadist will never go to Hell.

B4,52,66 Mohammed: "Anyone who gets his feet dirty while participating in jihad will not go to Hell."

B1,10,510 Mohammed: "If the heat of the day becomes oppressive, wait until it cools and say the Zuhr prayer. The heat you feel is from the raging fires of Hell."

Abu Talib was Mohammed's uncle and protector during his stay in Mecca. Without Abu Talib, Mohammed could not have been a prophet of Islam. He never converted to Islam, so all of his care and protection for Mohammed are with him in Hell.

B2,23,442 Mohammed went to see Abu Talib on his death-bed. As Abu Talib lay there with Abu and Abdullah attending, Mohammed said to him, "Uncle, for your sake say, 'There is only one god, Allah.' Before Allah I will bear witness to your conversion." Abu Jahl and Abdullah asked, "Abu Talib, will you forsake the religion of your ancestors?" While Mohammed continued to ask him to say, "There is only one God, Allah," Abu Jahl and Abdullah continued asking their question. Abu Talib's last words indicated that he still believed in the old religion, and he refused to say, "There is only one god, Allah."

Mohammed then said, "Unless Allah forbids me to do so, I will continue to ask him for your forgiveness." Consequently, Allah revealed this verse.

> 9:113 It is not for the Messenger or the faithful to pray for the forgiveness of Kafirs, even though they be of kin, after it has become clear to them that they are people of Hellfire.

More of Mohammed's generosity to Abu Talib, his protector.

B8,73,227 Abbas said, "Mohammed, did you try to protect Abu Talib from Allah's wrath the way he used to protect you from the anger of the Quraysh?" Mohammed said, "Yes, he is in the shallows of Hell. If not for me he would be in the deepest bowels of Hell."

B2,23,445 Mohammed said, "Anyone who willingly swears the truth of a lie by a religion other than Islam is damned to be what he has sworn. For example, if a man says, 'If I am lying, then I am a Jew,' then he actually is a Jew. If someone kills themselves with a steel blade, then punishment in Hell will be inflicted with the same blade."

Mohammed said, "A seriously injured man killed himself, so Allah said: 'My slave has brought about his death prematurely, therefore I forbid his entry into Paradise.'"

B2,23,468 After finishing morning prayers, Mohammed would turn to his followers and ask, "Did anyone have a dream last night?" Those who had dreams would describe them and Mohammed would say, "It is Allah's will." These dreams were considered good omens. One time, he asked if anyone had had a dream and everyone said no. Mohammed, however, said, "I had a dream where two men seized me by the hands and brought me to Jerusalem. I saw two men, one sitting and another standing with a big metal hook in his hand. The man with the hook pierced the cheek of the sitting man and tore it out, savagely ripping the flesh down to the bone. As the man with the hook was repeating the violence to the sitting man's other cheek, the injured cheek became as it was before. I asked, 'What does this mean?' The men told me to keep walking.

"Next we saw a man repeatedly smashing a rock onto the head of a man lying prone. Each time the rock crushed the one man's skull, it would roll away. The second man would retrieve the rock; return to the prone man, whose head had returned to normal; and he would repeat the procedure. I asked, "What does this mean?" The men merely told me to keep walking.

"Soon we came upon a hole with a wide bottom and a smaller top. It was some sort of furnace, and I could see nude men and women inside being buffeted about in the flames. As the flames flared up, the people inside the were propelled toward the top of the oven and the small opening. Before any could escape the flames, however, the inferno would slacken and the people would descend back into the depths of the fire. I asked, 'What does this mean?' The men just told me to keep walking.

"We walked until we came to a man standing in a river of blood. Each time the man attempted to climb out of the river, however, another man standing on the bank would throw a rock into his mouth forcing him back into the river. I asked, 'What does this mean?' The men simply told me to keep walking.

"We soon came to a beautiful and lush garden with a large tree and an old man and several children sitting beneath. Another man was nearby tending a fire. My guides made me climb and enter a house, finer than any I had ever seen. Inside the house there were several people, old and young men, and women and children.

"The two men led me from the house and again forced me to climb the tree and enter yet another house, even finer than the first. I said to the men, 'You have led me about all night. What does it all mean?' They said, 'We will explain. The man whose cheeks were being savaged was a liar upon whom the people relied. Consequently, his lies were spread across the land. That is his punishment until Judgment Day.'

"'The man whose head was crushed is someone who knew the Koran, but refused to recite it, or to act upon its teachings. The naked men and women in the furnace were adulterers. The man in the river of blood practiced usury. The old man sitting beneath the tree was Abraham and the young children were the descendents of the people. The man in the guarding tending the fire was Malik, the gate-keeper of Hell. The first house you entered was the house of believers, while the second house was the house of Martyrs. We are Gabriel and Michael. Lift up your head.' I lifted my head to the sky and saw what appeared to be a cloud. They said to me, 'That is your place in Paradise.' I replied, 'Let me enter and take my place.' They said, 'You have not yet completed your life. When you have completed your life you may enter and take your place.'"

ON SUICIDE

B7,71,670 Mohammed: "Anyone that deliberately jumps from a mountain and commits suicide will spend eternity falling in the depths of Hell. Anyone that kills themselves with poison will spend eternity in Hell drinking the same deadly mixture. Anyone that commits suicide with a blade will spend eternity in Hell stabbing themselves in the stomach."

B4,55,551 Mohammed: "Allah will ask the person receiving Hell's least punishment, 'If it were yours to give, would you give the world to ransom your freedom from Hell?' The man would say, 'Of course.' Allah will respond, 'When you were still part of Adam, I asked much less of you, specifically, I asked you to not worship any other except me, but you refused.'"

PARADISE

There are many hadiths about Hell. Very little is said about Paradise.

B4,54,469 Mohammed: "The first group of people entering Paradise will shine like the full moon; the next group will enter gleaming like the

North Star. Their hearts will be as one because there will be no strife among them. Everyone will have two beautiful wives, so radiant, chaste and transparent that the marrow of their leg bones will be visible through their skin. They will glorify Allah morning and night. They will forever remain in perfect health, never spitting or blowing their noses. Their tools will be made of silver and gold, as will be their combs, and their fires will burn aloe-wood and their perspiration will be perfumed musk."

This is the Sunna of Mohammed

CONCLUSIONS

CHAPTER 21

9:63 Do they not know that whoever opposes Allah
and His Messenger will abide in the Fire of Hell, where
they will remain forever? This is the great shame.

DUALITY

The Hadith divides humanity into two groups, Muslims and Kafirs. The Koran and the Sira present this same world view.

Each group has a different set of ethics so we call this dual ethics. There is one set that tells how to treat the Muslims and a second that describes how to treat the Kafir.

Non-Muslims can be treated kindly or they can be treated as the enemy of Allah. Their goods can be taken; they can be insulted, enslaved, raped and murdered if such treatment will advance Islam.

POLITICAL DUALITY

The Hadith contain the Sunna of jihad, slavery, dhimmis, and apostates. These are political issues with an ethical foundation. The suffering caused by jihad, slavery, dhimmis, and the killing of apostates is all based upon dualistic Islamic ethics. It is an absolute ethical inequality that is divine, sanctioned by the only god of the universe, Allah. This inequality between Muslim and Kafir is permanent and universal. It cannot be changed, reformed, or modified.

A Kafir is never the equal of a Muslim. Islam may respect a Kafir but can never accept him as equal.

The Koran, Hadith, and Sira are emphatic. The the only politics that can exist are the politics of Islam. Non-Muslims' politics are subject to the violence of jihad if the Kafirs do not submit. All governments must rule by Islamic Sharia law to achieve the peace of Islam.

UNITARY AND DUAL ETHICS

Unitary ethics are based upon the principle that at some fundamental level, all people are the same humanity, although they are not necessarily equal, as all people do not have the same abilities. This "sameness" means that we all want to be treated fairly. The perfect unitary ethical statement is: "Treat others as you wish to be treated." "Others" here means all of humanity is to be treated the same. This is an ideal perhaps, but failure to act upon it does not detract from its principle.

Dualistic Ethics

Give good advice to every Muslim.

A Muslim is a brother to every Muslim.

A Muslim is one who avoids harming any Muslim with his tongue or hands.

Unitary Ethics

Give good advice to every person.

A person is a brother to every person.

A person avoids harming any person with his tongue or hands.

The dual ethics of Islam are not as simple as having separate ethics for the Kafir. What makes political Islam so effective is that it has two stages of ethics for the Kafir, the ethics of the Meccan Koran and the ethics of the Medinan Koran. Islam can treat the Kafir well but as an inferior (Mecca) or treat him as an enemy of Allah (Medina). Both actions are sanctioned as sacred in the Koran. Muslims usually refer to the Meccan ethics when speaking to Kafirs. Apologists declare that the Meccan ethical system is the "real" Islam and that reform is possible.

Consider the comparisons between unitary and dualistic ethics in the table on the next page. These differences are not compatible. There is no middle ground or compromise between dualism and unitary ethics. They are mutually exclusive. Coexistence is temporary and when Islam is weak.

ISLAM AND AESTHETICS

Islamic aesthetics are clearly laid out in the Hadith. Art and the artist must submit to Islam. Mohammed, the divine perfect pattern for all humanity, clearly established that freedom and artistic expression are subject to Islam. All art—painting, sculpture, poetry, music, drama—is controlled by Sharia law. Art and artists that do not submit may be destroyed to please Allah.

Table 21.1: IDEALS OF DUALISM AND UNITARY ETHICS

THE MECCAN IDEALS OF DUALISM	THE MEDINAN IDEALS OF DUALISM	THE IDEALS OF UNITARY ETHICS
Islam is the religion of peace. A real Muslim is never violent.	Violence and threats are used against Kafirs. The violence is caused by the Kafirs failure to submit to Islam.	Peace is the desired state between groups.
Artists and intellectuals are pressured.	Artists and intellectuals that offend Islam are threatened and/or killed. Art and ideas must submit to Islam.	Artists and intellectuals are free to speak.
Islam is the "brother" religion of the Jews and Christians.	All religions must submit to Islam.	All religions are tolerated.
Demands are made on the host culture to accommodate Islam.	Differences are settled by threats and force (any compromise is temporary).	Differences are settled by negotiation and compromise.
Local laws are obeyed outside the Islamic community.	Islamic law (Sharia) is supreme. Kafirs are second class citizens.	All people are equal before the law.
Islam's poverty is caused by the Kafirs.	Islam takes wealth as its due.	Wealth is generated and created.

DUALISM AND THE RELIGION OF ISLAM

The statement that defines Islam, "There is no god but Allah, and Mohammed is his final prophet" is a dualistic statement.

Islam does not simply say Allah is the One-God. Why? Without Mohammed there is no Islam. To worship Allah, the One-God, does not make you a Muslim. Humanity must worship Allah exactly as Mohammed did. Only by worshipping the One-God, Allah, the way Mohammed did can make you a Muslim. It takes Allah and Mohammed to make Islam. A Muslim must be a Mohammedan. (Note: a Mohammedan no more worships Mohammed than a Confucian worships Confucius.)

The Kafir has no need for concern about the Paradise and Hell of Allah. What is of concern is how a secularist, a Christian, a Hindu, a Jew, or any other Kafir will be treated today, not after death.

STATISTICS AND THE TRILOGY

Jihad is systemically developed throughout all the Trilogy texts. The Hadith is 21% devoted to jihad.[1] Some apologists claim that there is a "greater jihad" that is spiritual struggle and that the killing jihad is the "lesser jihad".

But a textual count shows that 1.7% of all jihad hadiths are devoted to religious jihad. So the greater jihad of religion is smaller than 2% of Bukhari's jihad hadith text and the lesser jihad of the sword are 98%[2].

FIGURE 21.1: AMOUNT OF TEXT DEVOTED TO JIHAD

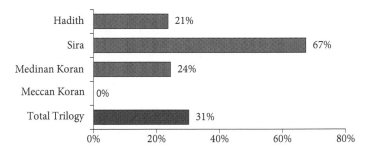

FIGURE 21.2: AMOUNT OF TEXT DEVOTED TO KAFIR

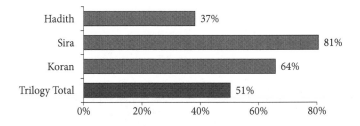

The graph above shows how much material is devoted to the Kafir[3]. The trilogy is over half about the Kafir, with the Hadith devoting 37% to language about the Kafir, all of it bad.

Religious Islam is defined as doctrine concerned with going to Paradise and avoiding Hell by following the Koran and the Sunna. The aspect of Islam that deals with the "outsider", the Kafir, is defined as political Islam. Since so much of the Trilogy, 51%, is about the Kafir, the

---

1   http://cspipublishing.com/statistical/TrilogyStats/Percentage_of_Trilogy_Text_Devoted_to_Jihad.html

2   http://cspipublishing.com/statistical/TrilogyStats/Greater-jihad.html

3   http://cspipublishing.com/statistical/TrilogyStats/AmtTxtDevotedKafir.html

statistical conclusion is that Islam is primarily a political system, not a religious system.

Mohammed's success depended on politics, not religion. The Sira, Mohammed's biography, gives a highly detailed accounting of his rise to power. He preached the religion of Islam for 13 years in Mecca and garnered 150 followers. He was forced to move to Medina and became a politician and warrior. During the last 9 years of his life, he was involved in an event of violence every 6 weeks. When he died every Arab was a Muslim. Mohammed succeeded through politics, not religion.

An estimate can be made that there were 100,000 Muslims[4] when Mohammed died. Using this information allows a graph to be drawn.

FIGURE 21.3: GROWTH OF ISLAM

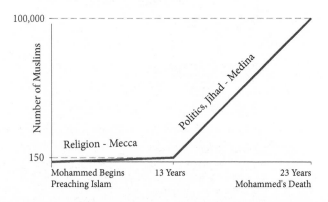

There are two distinct growth processes—religion and politics. Teaching and religion grew at a rate of about 12 new Muslims per year. Politics and jihad grew at a rate of 10,000 new Muslims per year, an enormous increase. This is a process yield improvement of over 800. Politics was roughly a thousand times more effective than religion.

If Mohammed had continued with preaching religion we can extrapolate that there would have only a few hundred Muslims when he died, instead of the 100,000 that resulted from his politics and jihad. This gives us an estimate of a few hundred conversions due to religion and over 99,000 conversions to due the political jihad process. We can calculate the relative contributions of religion and politics in growth.

---

4   *The History of al-Tabari*, volume XI, SUNY, Albany, NY, page 9.
Khalid, the sword of Allah, went into battle in 633 AD, with 10,000 Muslim Arab troops at the Battle of Chains. A nation at full conflict can field an army of about 10% of its population. If 10% is 10,000, then the total population is 100,000, a rough estimate.

Islam's success was less than 1% religion and over 99% politics at the time of Mohammed's death, 632 AD.

This graph is a very strong indicator of how effective politics was to establish Islam and how religion, alone, was a failure.

The entire Trilogy text has a great deal of Jew hatred material[5]. However, in the Meccan Koran there is very little. But the Hadith alone has more Jew hatred than *Mein Kampf*.

FIGURE 21.4: ANTI-JEWISH TEXT IN TRILOGY

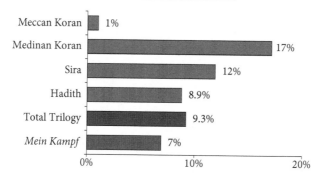

The Hadith's treatment of women is of interest[6]. This chart was prepared by collecting all of the hadiths that include any mention of women. These are then sorted into neutral, low status, high status and equal status. The neutral verses are not included in the study.

Equal status occurs on judgment day when men and women will be held accountable for their actions. High status comes from being a mother. In every other way women are subjugated.

FIGURE 21.5: STATUS OF WOMEN IN THE HADITH (331 HADITHS)

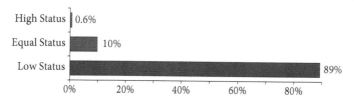

5 http://cspipublishing.com/statistical/TrilogyStats/Amt_anti-Jew_Text.html

6 http://cspipublishing.com/statistical/TrilogyStats/Womans_Status_in_the_Hadith.html

THE FOUNDATIONALIST SCHOOL

The actions and words of Muslims have their foundation in the doctrine of Islam found in the Koran, the Sira and the Hadith, the Islamic Trilogy. This doctrine must be analyzed and understood on a rational basis and on its own merits. Know the foundational doctrine of Islam and apply it to every action by Muslims, but first know the doctrine.

The Foundationalist school is fact-based and scientific. It posits a cause and effect relationship between Islamic doctrine and the behavior and speech of Muslims. If an opinion or comment about Islam does not have a reference, or a possible reference, to the Trilogy, then the opinion has no merit.

The Foundationalist school sees Islamic history as being the fruit of its doctrine. Since both past and present Islam are based upon the same unchanging doctrine, it is possible to understand from the actions of Muslims today what the future will bring.

****

You have just finished reading excerpts from a sacred text. The next time you read a news account of Islam, stop and consider how Islam's actions are always based upon the Hadith and the rest of the Trilogy.

Now that you have been introduced to the Hadith, go to a Web site and read in detail the original documents. Enter the word *hadith* in your browser and select one of the many sites that give the full collections. They are fascinating.

FOR MORE INFORMATION

www.politicalislam.com
www.cspii.com
Facebook: @BillWarnerAuthor
Twitter: @politicalislam.com
You Tube: Political Islam

BIBLIOGRAPHY

Watt, W. Montgomery and Bell, Richard. *Introduction to the Quran.* Edinburgh: Edinburgh University Press, 1970.

Robinson, Neal. *Discovering the Koran.* London: SCM Press, 1996.

Arberry, A. J. *The Koran Interpreted*, NY: Touchstone, 1996.

Pickthall, Mohammed M. *The Meaning of the Glorious Koran.* Kuwait: Dar al-Islamiyya.

Warraq, Ibn. *What the Koran Really Says.* Amherst, NY: Prometheus Books, 2002.

Dawood, N. J. *The Koran*, London: Penguin Books, 1999.

Rodwell, J. M. *The Koran*, North Clarendon, VT: Tuttle Publishing, 1994.

Ali, Maulana Muhammad. *Holy Koran.* Columbus, Ohio: Ahmadiyyah Anjuman Ishaat Islam 1998.

Watt, W. Montgomery and M.V. McDonald. *The History of al-Tabari, vol. VI, Muhammad at Mecca.* New York: The State University of New York Press, 1987.

McDonald, M.V. and W. Montgomery Watt. *The History of al-Tabari, vol. VII, The Foundation of the Community.* New York: The State University of New York Press, 1987.

Michael Fishbone, *The History of al-Tabari VIII The Victory of Islam.* New York: The State University of New York Press, 1987.

Poonawala, Ismail K. *The History of al-Tabari, vol. IX, The Last Years of the Prophet.* New York: The State University of New York Press, 1987.

Muir, Sir William. *Life of Mohammed.* New York: AMS Press, 1975.

Guillaume, A. *The Life of Muhammad*, (Ishaq's—Sirat Rasul Allah). Karachi: Oxford University Press, 1967.

Khan, Muhammad M. *The Translation of the Meanings of Sahih Al-Bukhari: Arabic-English.* Riyadh, Darussalam, 1997

J.H. Worcester: *The Life of David Livingstone.* Woman's Presbyterian Board of Missions of the Northwest. Chicago. 1888.

INDEX

Z

Made in the USA
Middletown, DE
20 September 2017